One Hundred and One Reasons Why We Are Baptized

The Foundation Covenant

Philip M. Hudson

Copyright 2018 by Philip M. Hudson.
The book author retains sole copyright
to his contributions to this book.

Published 2018.
Printed in the United States of America.

All rights reserved.

No portion of this book may be reproduced, stored in a retrieval system, or transmitted in any form or by any means – electronic, mechanical, photocopy, recording, scanning, or other – except for brief quotations in critical reviews or articles, without the prior written permission of the author.

ISBN 978-1-943650-80-4

Library of Congress Control Number 2018948093

Illustrations – Google Images.

This book may be ordered from
online bookstores.

Published by BookCrafters
Parker, Colorado.
www.bookcrafters.net

Table of Contents

- Preface...i
- Introduction...v
- One Through One Hundred and One...1
- One Hundred and Two Through One Hundred and Thirty Eight........................102
- Appendix 1: One Hundred and One Reasons Why We Are Baptized..................141
- Appendix 2: An Additional Three Dozen Reasons...147
- Appendix 3: Discussion Questions..149
- Appendix 4: Baptismal Prayers in The Standard Works.....................................221
- Appendix 4: The Fourth Article of Faith..223
- Appendix 5: Bible Dictionary (Baptism)...225
- Appendix 6: Topical Guide (Baptism)..229
- Appendix 7: Brigham Young's Testimony Relating to His Baptism.....................233
- Appendix 8: Lorenzo Snow's Testimony Relating to His Baptism......................235
- Appendix 9: Phil Hudson's Testimony of Baptism...237
- Author's Note..241
- About The Author..243
- Also By The Author..245

Preface

"Behold, he changed their hearts; yea, he awakened them out of a deep sleep, and they awoke unto God. Behold, they were in the midst of darkness; nevertheless, their souls were illuminated by the light of the everlasting word."
(Alma 5:7).

This book was inspired by the capacity of baptism to change our hearts. Those who have come up out of the world to join the Church in our day via the portal of baptism know how the people of Zarahemla felt, when they exclaimed to their prophet Benjamin: "We believe all the words which thou hast spoken unto us; and also, we know of their surety and truth, because of the Spirit of the Lord Omnipotent, which has wrought a mighty change in us, or in our hearts, that we have no more disposition to do evil, but to do good continually." (Mosiah 5:2).

Alma posed a rhetorical question to those who had been rejuvenated in the refreshing waters of baptism: "Have ye spiritually been born of God?" he asked. "Have ye received his image in your countenances? Have ye experienced this mighty change in your hearts?" (Alma 5:14). Then, by extension, he continued: "If ye have experienced a change of heart, and if ye have felt to sing the song of redeeming love, I would ask, can ye feel so now?" (Alma 5:26). This book has been written not only to prepare our friends and neighbors, and our little children for baptism, but also to help those of us who have long since entered the healing waters to sustain the feelings we then experienced.

In the physical world, although we may have previously enjoyed active lifestyles, our hearts sometimes begin to falter. They may skip a beat or two now and then, or we may suffer from arrhythmia (an abnormal heart rhythm), tachycardia (an abnormally rapid heart rate), or bradycardia (an abnormally slow heart rate). We may experience shortness of breath, or suffer from angina, the chest pain that is related to insufficient oxygenated blood reaching the heart muscle. When we exhibit the symptoms of heart disease, we are quick to initiate protocols designed to restore function. We make dietary changes, go to a gym, take the stairs instead of the elevator, and modify other habit patterns. We read everything we can about the subject, and follow the counsel of experts in the fields of medicine, physical therapy, and biofeedback. We seek inspiration from lifestyle coaches and self-help gurus. We learn how to monitor our cardiovascular health, and we establish benchmarks to more easily gauge our progress toward the achievement of our goals. When we re-establish sustainable levels of fitness, we eschew the poor lifestyle choices that had aforetime compromised our health, and now would threaten to abrogate our gains.

There is a spiritual equivalent to the healthy lifestyle protocols that are initiated to address heart disease. Baptism is a doctrinal digitalis that has the capacity to "lift up (and strengthen our) hearts (that we might) be glad." (D&C 29:5). Those who decline the invitation to be baptized, however, risk being left with heavy hearts that bear the weight of wickedness. When their lives are in commotion, surely their hearts shall fail them. (See D&C 88:91).

Before the foundation of the world, Heavenly Father knew that His children would need a powerful antidote to the physical and spiritual assaults on the integrity of their hearts that would be a part of the opposition in all things required by the principle of free will that is integral to the Plan of Salvation. Because "they that be whole need not a physician, but they that are sick," baptism was instituted in the lone and dreary world as the spiritual equivalent of powerful heart medication, surgical implants, and even organ transplants, that are required to address the cardiomyopathy of compromised hearts. (Luke 5:31).

When the children of God have forsaken the world and have embraced the lifestyle of saints, they experience in baptism a figurative organ transplant procedure. Those who have literally had heart transplants find it necessary to adhere to a cocktail of immuno-suppressant medication, following a strict regimen, for the rest of their lives. The same prescription must be taken, in a specific dose, at the same time every day. The routine must be followed without variation, in order to maintain a homeostatic balance that minimizes the risk of failure of the surgical procedure. All doctor's appointments must be kept, every recommended laboratory test must be performed, medication side effects must be monitored, and drug interactions and the signs and symptoms of organ rejection must be managed.

The same anti-rejection protocols must be followed after we have spiritually changed our hearts and have been born again through baptism. As the prophet Ezekiel declared: "A new heart also will I give you, and a new spirit will I put within you: and I will take away the stony heart out of your flesh, and I will give you an heart of flesh." (Ezekiel 36:26).

If we are not vigilant, however, our new hearts will surely fail us. Our heaven-sent immuno-suppressant medication comes in the form of prayer, service, and temple attendance. Our strict regimen takes the shape of regular church attendance. Our diligence with medication is manifest in the ordinances of the Gospel, and our determination to maintain heart-healthy lifestyle choices includes the bread and water that is offered on a weekly basis during our ward Sacrament services.

We are meticulous to keep our appointments with our spiritual physicians, and we look forward to the house calls represented in visits by ministering brothers and sisters. We take advantage of accountability interviews with our ward and stake leaders. We are alert to our need for regularly recurring repentance and are sensitive to the spiritual promptings that assure us that we have received forgiveness of our sins and are on the path of progress. If we sense that our organ transplant has begun to fail, or if we feel that it is being rejected because of the insidious effects of carnality, sensuality, or devilishness, we hasten to the temple, for we know to Whom we must turn for guidance and direction, so that we might be able to once again sing the song of redeeming love that comes with spiritual heart health.

We put our shoulders to the wheel, and push along. We tailor ministering messages to the changing needs of our brothers and sisters. We cycle through the Standard Works in Sunday School class every four years, even if for no other reason than that we need to maintain a high level of fitness on the stationary bicycle of belief. If our efforts seem repetitive, it may just be that the Choreographer of the universe is interested in theatrical encore.

Baptism is not pedestrian, but is spectacular; it is not dreary, but is dramatic; and it is not uninteresting, but is stimulating. It quietly establishes a habit pattern of obedience designed to last a lifetime. Baptism is of such magnitude, and has such an outward and upward thrust, that it can reap rewards that reach all the way into eternity.

Following our baptism, critics who focus only on physical fitness, while neglecting spiritual strength, might see only frivolous repetition in the efforts of baptized members of the Church to maintain spiritually aerobic health. They confuse the philosophies of men mingled with scripture, for the Doctrine of Christ. In fact, those of us who have undergone the spiritual heart transplant of baptism, enjoy an indescribable moment in the sun, when the light of understanding illuminates our minds and confirms the divine potential of the new organ beating steadily in our chest.

By remembering our covenant of baptism, we enjoy a gift that keeps on giving, as our new hearts beat 80 times per minute, 4,800 times per hour, and 115,200 times per day. To the Lord, all things are spiritual, and not at any time has He given us laws that are temporal. (See D&C 29:324). We remember this, as, over the course of a year, our new hearts beat over 42 million times. In 70 years, that's almost 3 billion beats. Baptism has the capacity to pump the spiritual element through 100,000 miles of blood vessels in our circulatory systems, 2,000 gallons of it daily, 730,000 gallons per year, or up to 51,000,000 gallons in 70 years.

Every day of our lives, as the sunrise breaks over the eastern sky, the self-evident question is unequivocally answered with our baptism and in the subsequent conduct of our lives: "What think ye of Christ? Whose son is he?" (Matthew 22:42).

Our discipline weaves a tapestry that testifies we have been born again to enjoy one more day on earth. We are fortified in baptism to meet our most daunting challenges. Our new hearts almost burst with the spiritual element that sustains our forward momentum, as we push on toward the unexplored reaches of eternity. We realize that our baptism has not only the capacity to improve our lifestyle, but also that it taps into God's power to sustain our very lives. He has provided a marvelous opportunity for us to probe the limits of our potential and to enjoy spiritual stability. Our baptism casts us off into a stream of revelation, that we might be carried along in the quickening currents of direct experience with the Infinite.

Introduction

Gospel principles are the foundation truths that are embedded in doctrine. They are eternally valid, while values are beliefs that are culturally or personally determined, and that may change with circumstances. Baptism is an excellent example of an ordinance that is the expression of a Gospel principle.

Baptism amplifies the quiet spiritual stirrings that underlie our experience, and is a portal opening up into the matchless vistas of spiritual experience. There are no social, economic, cultural, environmental, or genealogical prerequisites that limit who may receive its blessings. The only real condition for receiving the priesthood ordinance of baptism is bringing "forth fruit meet for repentance." (Alma 13:13).

The repentant, Joseph Smith said, are "baptized after the manner of his burial, being buried in the water in his name, and this according to the commandment which he has given – That by keeping the commandments they might be washed and cleansed from all their sins." (D&C 76:51-52). "Consequently, the baptismal font was instituted as a similitude of the grave." (D&C 128:13).

Paul taught that being immersed in water and coming out again is symbolic of both death and resurrection. He wrote: "Therefore, we are buried with him by baptism into death: that like as Christ was raised up from the dead by the glory of the Father, even so we also should walk in newness of life. For if we have been planted together in the likeness of his death, we shall be also in the likeness of his resurrection." (Romans 6:4).

He also taught that there is "one Lord, one faith, (and) one baptism." (Ephesians 4:5). There was no disputation regarding the correct administration of the ordinance of baptism as long as the Apostles walked the earth. When they were martyred, however, and their priesthood authority died with them, confusion arose concerning the simplest policies, procedures, and doctrines of the kingdom, and there was no enlightened solution to the problem. Apostasy resulted, that only ended with the direct latter day intervention in the Sacred Grove by Heavenly Father and His Son Jesus Christ. (See J.S.H. 1:16-20).

Paul had prophesied of the coming apostasy from the faith. He wrote to the saints: "Be not soon shaken in mind, or be troubled, neither by spirit, nor by word, nor by letter as from us, as that the day of Christ is at hand. Let no man deceive you by any means: for that day shall not come, except there come a falling away first." (2 Thessalonians 2:2-3).

In the third century A.D., the Church historian Eusebius provided a glimpse of that falling away. He wrote: "A change came over us. We yielded to pride, sloth, mutual envy, and abuse. We warred upon ourselves as occasion offered, and we used the weapons of words. Leaders fought and laity formed factions. Unspeakable hypocrisy and dissimulation traveled to the farthest limits of evil." ("The Essential Eusebius," p. 177).

Later, during the Age of Chivalry, Charlemagne urged churchmen to faithful Gospel scholarship. "In a letter to abbots and bishops, he complained of illiterate monks: 'What pious devotion had faithfully prompted in their hearts, their uneducated tongues could not put into words without stumbling.' Hardly a Bible existed that was not riddled with the gross errors of untutored copyists." (Will Durant, "The Age of Chivalry," p. 61).

A leader of the Reformation in America, Roger Williams, wrote: "There is no regularly constituted church on earth, nor any person authorized to administer any church ordinance (such as baptism); nor can there be until new apostles are sent by the Great Head of the Church, for Whose coming I am seeking." ("Picturesque America," p. 502, see also the 5th Article of Faith).

Finally, Thomas Jefferson fumed that "the religion builders have so distorted and deformed the doctrines of Jesus, so muffled them in mysticisms, fancies, and falsehoods, have caricatured them into forms so inconceivable, as to shock reasonable thinkers. Happy in the prospect of a restoration of primitive Christianity, I must leave to younger persons to encounter and lop off the false branches that have been engrafted into it by the mythologists of the middle and modern ages." ("Jefferson's Complete Works," 7:210 & 257).

The Restoration reestablished the necessity of the ordinance of baptism and reinstated the authority to act in the name of God. Anciently, Christ gave the Nephite Twelve the specific words that they were to employ in the baptismal prayer, so that there might be no misunderstanding. Because this prayer authorizes the officiant to invoke the Holy Names of all three members of the Godhead, its words convey unmatched power, and suggest, without reservation, the sanction and approval of God Himself.

We must be baptized for the remission of sins because the principle upon which the ordinance is anchored is based on a commandment found throughout the canon of scripture: "Repent, and be baptized every one of you in the name of Jesus Christ for the remission of sins." (Acts 2:38). In the scriptures, Jesus Himself, and little children, are the only perfect examples. He said: "Ye must repent, and be baptized in my name, and become as a little child, or ye can in nowise inherit the kingdom of God." (3 Nephi 11:38).

We must be baptized to become members of the Church of Jesus Christ. "All those who humble themselves before God, and desire to be baptized (that) have truly repented of all their sins...shall be received by baptism into his church." (D&C 20:37). In a beautiful admonition, Alma described 14 key qualities that Latter-day Saints should have as they come out of the waters of baptism. "Be humble," he said, "and be submissive and gentle; easy to be entreated; full of patience and long-suffering; being temperate in all things; being diligent in keeping the commandments of God at all times; asking for whatsoever things ye stand in need, both spiritual and temporal, always returning thanks unto God for whatsoever things ye do receive. And see that ye have faith, hope, and charity, and then will ye always abound in good works." (Alma 7:23-24). The characteristics of the Zion society he envisioned are simply the result of a spiritual transformation that takes place as the saints live the Celestial Law of the Lord.

We must be baptized that we might walk in the light of the Spirit, and not just of the Light of Christ. "If thou wilt turn unto me, and (be baptized) ye shall receive the gift of the Holy Ghost." (Moses 6:52). As we participate in the ordinance of the Sacrament in renewal of the baptismal covenant, and so live that the Holy Ghost may be our Companion, we will be guided unerringly.

Brigham Young declared: "Every individual that lives according to the laws that the Lord has given to His people, and has received the blessings that He has in store for the faithful, should be able to know the things of God from the things which are not of God, the light from the darkness, that which comes from heaven and that which comes from somewhere else. This is the satisfaction and the consolation that the Latter-day Saints enjoy by living their religion. This is the knowledge which every one who thus lives possesses." (D.B.Y., p. 35).

Following his own baptism, Joseph Smith wrote: "Our minds being now enlightened, we began to have the scriptures laid open to our understandings, and the true meaning and intention of their more mysterious passages revealed unto us in a manner which we never could attain to previously, nor ever before had thought of." (J.S.H. 1:74).

We are baptized that we might follow in the footsteps of the Savior. Obedience frees us from the uncertainties of mortality. Joseph F. Smith taught that we need not fear in our hearts when we have lived up to the principles of truth and righteousness, according to our knowledge and understanding.

The Savior, Who was our Exemplar, both physically and symbolically descended beneath us all, when He was baptized in Jordan, which is the lowest body of fresh water upon the face of the earth. In our own day, "persecutions may rage, mobs may combine, armies may assemble, calumny may defame, but the truth of God will go forth boldly, nobly, and independent," proclaimed by baptized members of the Lord's missionary army, "until it has penetrated every continent, visited every clime, swept every country, and sounded in every ear, till the purposes of God shall be accomplished and the Great Jehovah shall say 'The work is done.'" (Joseph Smith, H.C. 4:540).

Although telestial turf is Satan's home ground, and the quicksand of secular humanism and other false ideologies lies ready to suck the unwary into the underworld of the adversary, "no power on earth or hell can overthrow or defeat that which God has decreed. Every plan of the adversary will fail, for the Lord knows our secret thoughts and sees the future with a vision clear and perfect, even as though it were in the past." (Joseph Fielding Smith, Jr.).

Baptism is the gateway through which we enter as we embark on the path of eternal progress leading to the Celestial Kingdom. The Savior promised: "Whoso believeth in me, and is baptized...shall inherit the kingdom of God." (3 Nephi 11:33). Those who are baptized "have come out of the world, have left the loneliness and estrangement of a fallen creation, and have entered the realm of divine experience. They have forsaken the orphanage of spiritual alienation, and have been received into the family and household of the Lord Jesus Christ. They have left the ranks of the nameless, and have taken upon them the blessed name of Jesus Christ. They are Christians. Through their Master, they become, in time, joint heirs to all that the Father has." (Doctrinal Commentary on The Book of Mormon," 4:202). Referring to those who lived following the post-mortal ministry of the Savior among the Nephites, Mormon simply exclaimed: "How blessed were they!" (4 Nephi 1:18).

In contrast, those who do not believe in the power of God unto salvation, and are not baptized, will not be able to continue their progression, and will therefore be damned. This is not an arbitrary man-made judgment with corollaries, footnotes, and exceptions to the rule. God's laws are not subject to appeal, amendment, or interpretation. Baptism is the key element of a perfect Plan that is all the more beautiful because of its simplicity. The ordinance is clearly established in the Bible and is clarified in companion scriptures. It's administration is carefully articulated in The Book of Mormon to silence doctrinal disputations among the people. It is the ordinance that is central to The Plan of Salvation, and is the hinge upon which swings the gate leading to eternal life with Heavenly Father.

As King Benjamin so clearly taught: "Under this head ye are made free, and there is no other head whereby ye can be made free. There is no other name given whereby salvation cometh; therefore, I would that ye should take upon you the name of Christ, all you that have entered into the covenant with God that ye should be obedient unto the end of your lives. And it shall come to pass that whosoever doeth this shall be found at the right hand of God, for he shall know the name by which he is called; for he shall be called by the name of Christ. And now it shall come to pass, that whosoever shall not take upon him the name of Christ must be called by some other name; therefore, he findeth himself on the left hand of God." (Mosiah 5:8-10).

Benjamin's discourse expressed a divine perspective. It echoed the prophets, who from the foundation of the world have clarified again and again the first principles and ordinances of the Gospel Plan. When we hear the Lord's anointed repeating themselves, we need to perk up our ears and listen carefully, for "surely the Lord God will do nothing, but he revealeth his secret unto his servants the prophets." (Amos 2:7).

All who have reached the age of accountability are invited to be baptized. At that age, we are old enough to comprehend covenants with our Creator. Almost a year before the formal organization of the Church, the Lord taught Joseph Smith that we must repent "if we have arrived at the years of accountability," (D&C 18:42), that elsewhere is specified as the age of eight. (See D&C 68:27).

All those who have reached the age of accountability have been guided by the light of Christ to establish the foundation of an understanding of what is good and what is evil. (See 2 Nephi 9:25-26). Because of the Atonement, all have equal opportunity before the Lord, and baptism becomes the powerful ordinance it was meant to be. Ultimately, we may all "have the privilege, living or dead, of accepting the conditions of the great Plan of Redemption provided by the Father, through the Son, before the world was." (John Taylor, "Mediation and Atonement," p. 181).

Baptism helps to make our lives a time of testing, or of putting to the proof our declared values. It gives us a new beginning, which is why it is called a rebirth. If we are baptized after we have reached the age of accountability, we are freed from the stain of sin that has been accumulating since that time. "Inasmuch as ye were born into the world by water, and blood, and the spirit, which I have made, and so became of dust a living soul, even so ye must be born again into the kingdom of heaven, of water, and of the Spirit, and be cleansed by blood, even the blood of mine Only Begotten." (Moses 6:59).

The covenant of baptism is a two-way promise. We make a covenant with the Lord to come into the fold of God, to bear each other's burdens, to stand as His witnesses at all times and in all places, and to serve Him and keep His commandments. In turn, the Lord promises to forgive our sins, to pour out His Spirit more abundantly upon us, to give us daily guidance and help, with a promise that we will come forth in the First Resurrection, and be rewarded with eternal life.

The intensity of the ordinance allows us to discover for ourselves the very personal levels of the experiences of the Savior. When He speaks of "knowing Him," the Savior is referring to a special sense of the word. It is not enough that we know about Him, by reading the Gospels, or by listening to others speak of Him. We must know Him through the bonds of common experience and common feeling. Our baptism was meant to be an immersion in the tangible element of Spirit.

We can feel as did the Dead Sea Covenanters, who wrote of their baptismal experience: "His sin is forgiven him and in the humility of his soul he is for all the Laws of God; his flesh is cleansed shining bright in the waters of purification, even in the waters of baptism, and he shall be given a new name in due time to walk perfect in all the ways of God." ("The Manual of Discipline" or "The Serek Scroll" from The Dead Sea Scrolls).

Melvin J. Ballard was one who, following his baptism, was able to walk perfectly in all the ways of God. He said: "I found myself one evening in the dreams of the night in the sacred building, the temple. After a season of prayer and rejoicing, I was informed that I should have the privilege of entering into one of those rooms, to meet a glorious Personage, and, as I entered the door, I saw, seated on a raised platform, the most glorious Being my eyes have ever beheld or that I ever conceived existed in all the eternal worlds. As I approached to be introduced, he arose and stepped towards me with extended arms and he smiled as he softly spoke my name. If I shall live to be a million years old, I shall never forget that smile. He took me in his arms and kissed me, pressed me to his bosom and blessed me, until the marrow of my bones seemed to melt. When he had finished, I fell at his feet, and as I bathed them with my tears and kisses, I saw the prints of the nails in the feet of the Redeemer of the world. The feeling that I had in the presence of Him who hath all things in His hands, to have His love, His affection and His blessing was such that if I ever can receive that of which I had but a foretaste, I would give all I am, all that I ever hope to be, to feel what I then felt." ("Sermons and Missionary Experiences of Melvin Joseph Ballard," p. 156).

Mormon desired that his brethren might have similar cherished relationships with the Lord, and so he found it necessary to speak to his son about a practice that had crept into the Church that grieved him tremendously. He had learned that there had been disputations among his people concerning the baptism of their little children. (See Moroni 8:5).

There have always been such disputes. The practice of infant baptism in the various sects in the Last Days, and the differences of opinion regarding the correct method of the administration of baptism in Joseph Smith's day, made the Restoration of the Gospel necessary. The Atonement made the correct administration of the ordinance of baptism possible. It is critically important that the sacred ordinance admitting an applicant into the fold of Christ be carried out according to His instruction, for, as noted above, there is ultimately "one Lord, one faith, (and only) one baptism." (Ephesiahs 4:5). "Except a man be born of water and of the Spirit," declared the Savior, "he cannot enter into the kingdom of God." (John 3:5).

Even in the days of the patriarchs, there was confusion concerning the proper administration of the ordinance of baptism. "And it came to pass, that Abram fell on his face, and called upon the name of the Lord. And God talked with him, saying, my people have gone astray from my precepts, and have not kept mine ordinances, which I gave unto their fathers. And they have not observed mine anointing, and the burial, or baptism wherewith I commanded them; but have turned from the commandment, and taken unto themselves the washing of children, and the blood of sprinkling; And have said that the blood of the righteous Abel was shed for sins; and have not known wherein they are accountable before me." (J.S.T. Genesis 17:3-7).

Mormon considered the dispute to be of such magnitude that immediately upon learning of it, he sought the advice of the Lord concerning the matter. The ecclesiastical counsel that he then gave came by direct revelation by the power of the Spirit, just as it has in the Last Days. The reason that a correct understanding of baptism is essential is that the ordinance lies at the very heart of the Gospel of Jesus Christ.

As the Savior taught the Nephites: "This is the gospel which I have given unto you - that I came into the world to do the will of my Father, because my Father sent me. And my Father sent me that I might be lifted up upon the cross; and after that I had been lifted up upon the cross, that I might draw all men unto me. ...And it shall come to pass, that whoso repenteth and is baptized in my name shall be filled. ...And he that endureth not unto the end, the same is he that is also hewn down and cast into the fire, from whence they can no more return, because of the justice of the Father." (3 Nephi 27:13-21).

Mormon had a correct understanding of the mission of the Redeemer, and knew that He had come "into the world not to call the righteous but sinners to repentance: the whole need no physician, but they that are sick; wherefore little children are whole, for they are not capable of committing sin. (Moroni 8:8). Therefore, he said, "It is solemn mockery before God, that ye should baptize little children," because to do so denies the far-reaching power of the Atonement. (Moroni 8:9).

The doctrine of infant baptism denies that Jesus Christ atoned for the "original sin" of Adam, and ignores the concept of individual accountability. It demands that little children who die without baptism cannot enter heaven. But the Atonement did redeem them from the Fall. They are capable of actions that are inconsistent with obedience to Gospel principles, but they are not counted against them as sins, for they are not culpable.

Rather, Mormon wrote: "This thing shall ye teach - repentance and baptism unto those who are accountable and capable of committing sin; yea, teach parents that they must repent and be baptized, and humble themselves as their little children, and they shall all be saved with their little children." (Moroni 8:10). Then, for added emphasis, he declared: "Little children need no repentance, neither baptism. Behold, baptism is unto repentance to the fulfilling the commandments unto the remission of sins. But little children are alive in Christ, even from the foundation of the world." (Moroni 8:11-12).

It was an integral part of The Plan of Salvation, ordained in the Grand Council in Heaven before the world was, that little children who died before the age of accountability would be saved in the Celestial Kingdom by the power of the Infinite Atonement. "If not so, God is a partial God, and also a changeable God, and a respecter of persons; for how many little children have died without baptism!" Moroni 8:22).

Those who labor under the burden of a belief in infant baptism are "in the gall of bitterness," for how could a just and loving Father in Heaven consign so many of His innocent children to an eternal fate which, on their own merits, they did not deserve?" (Moroni 8:14). These ignorant individuals are "in the bonds of iniquity" in the sense that they must experience despair or hopelessness regarding their little ones who have died without baptism. (Moroni 8:14).

"Despair cometh because of iniquity" because sin clouds vision, and unrepentant sinners can see no way out of their miserable situation. (Moroni 10:22). Apostate teaching leaves no alternative but to suggest, "if little children could not be saved without baptism, these must have gone to an endless hell." (Moroni 8:13).

It is those who persist in the practice of infant baptism, however, who "must go down to hell," wrote Mormon. (Moroni 8:14). While those who teach the doctrine of infant baptism believe that children who die without the ordinance will go to hell, the truth is that it is the professors of that doctrine who are themselves "in danger of death, hell, and an endless torment." (Moroni 8:21).

"For awful is the wickedness to suppose that God saveth one child because of baptism, and the other must perish because he hath no baptism. Wo be unto them that shall pervert the ways of the Lord after this manner, for (after they have been taught about the role of accountability following the fall of Adam, and the necessity of the Savior's redemption) they shall perish except they repent." (Moroni 8:15-16).

The scriptures are specific because our eternal welfare depends upon our correct understanding of this doctrine. All else hangs in the balance. At the end of the day, in the absence of sin, there is no need for repentance, or for baptism. This doctrine was established before the foundation of the world. "For the power of redemption cometh on all those that have no law; wherefore, he that is...under no condemnation cannot repent; and unto such baptism availeth nothing." (Mormon 822).

In a grand summary statement, Mormon concluded: "The first fruits of repentance is baptism; and baptism cometh by faith unto the fulfilling the commandments; and the fulfilling the commandments bringeth remission of sins; and the remission of sins bringeth meekness, and lowliness of heart; and because of meekness and lowliness of heart cometh the visitation of the Holy Ghost, which Comforter filleth with hope and perfect love, which love endureth by diligence unto prayer, until the end shall come, when all the saints shall dwell with God." (Moroni 8:25-26).

1000 years earlier, Nephi had written extensively regarding the doctrine of baptism. 2 Nephi Chapters 31-33 represent the culmination of his desire to persuade those living in the Last Days "to come unto the God of Abraham, and the God of Isaac, and the God of Jacob, and be saved." (1 Nephi 6:4). These chapters comprise Nephi's last recorded sermon, and address what he called "the doctrine of Christ." (2 Nephi 31:2). Simply stated, this doctrine is that if we have faith in Jesus Christ, repent of our sins, and enter into a baptismal covenant with the Lord, we will receive the Holy Ghost, Who will then guide us, showing us the things we must do to achieve salvation and exaltation.

Nephi emphasized that the Lord would be baptized "to fulfil all righteousness," which is to obey every commandment and to perform every ordinance necessary to attain eternal life. (2 Nephi 31:5). The doctrine of Christ speaks to our spirits, for every Gospel principle carries a witness that it is true. The language of the Spirit is universal, and when the Holy Ghost illuminates our minds, we enjoy spiritual fluency. Such familiarity, such ease with the doctrines, and such comfort with the revealed word of God, open up vistas of eternal proportion.

The Book of Mormon does not make any special mention of the manner of baptism among Nephi's contemporaries, for baptism had always been the standard for the Children of the Covenant. Five hundred years later in the Old World, when John the Baptist went into the wilderness of Judea preaching repentance and baptism by immersion, his actions didn't arouse any curiosity among the people, as if he were introducing some new and strange doctrine. The Jews of that day understood it as an essential Gospel ordinance, and so it was. Even the Jewish Encyclopedia states: "John stood forth in the spirit of the prophets of old to preach his baptism of repentance symbolized by cleansing with water." (Volume 2, p. 499).

"The fact that baptism was practiced in ancient Israel might (also) help to explain why the Savior was not criticized by the orthodox Jews who were quick to rebuke Him whenever He did anything contrary to their law. However, not a single word of criticism concerning the baptism of Jesus Christ is found in the entire New Testament." ("Commentary on The Book of Mormon," p. 155).

It is obvious that baptism is an ordinance of great antiquity, and one requiring humility and obedience before God the Father. The Lamb of God was indeed baptized, for Elder Howard W. Hunter declared: "Jesus entered into all the saving ordinances of the Melchizedek Priesthood," and baptism qualifies one to participate in these. (Los Angeles Area Conference Address, 1980).

The Savior's example demonstrated that entrance into the Church and Kingdom is strait; that is to say, it is narrowly defined. There should be no variance of opinion regarding the prescribed way. He set the pattern when He said: "Follow thou me." (2 Nephi 31:10). The ecclesiastical responsibility of the Lord's anointed has always been to teach correct principles. Witness the Latter-day prophets who pointedly invite less active members of the Church to return to the fold in full fellowship.

To a later Nephite society, the Savior Himself taught with unmistakable clarity. "And he said unto them: On this wise shall ye baptize; and there shall be no disputations among you." (3 Nephi 11:22). "Neither shall there be disputations among you concerning the points of my doctrine." (3 Nephi 11:28). There followed explicit instruction to the priesthood leaders of the Nephite Church regarding the manner of baptism. The history of post-apostolic Christianity bears witness that it is vitally important that the members of His Church be taught the Doctrine of Christ. As Nephi asked: "Wherefore, my beloved brethren, can we follow Jesus save we shall be willing to keep the commandments of the Father? And the Father said: Repent ye, repent ye, and be baptized in the name of my Beloved Son." (2 Nephi 31:10-11).

Baptism, then, serves many purposes. Among these, 1) It illustrates our desire to follow the righteous example of the Savior, 2) It is an expression of our obedience, 3) It allows us to receive a remission of sins, if we are baptized after the age of accountability, 4) It enables us to gain admission to the Church, through an ordinance performed by His legal administrators, 5) It provides us with access to personal sanctification through the Holy Ghost, and 6) It is outwardly symbolic as the gateway to the Celestial Kingdom of God. As this book illustrates, there are dozens of additional reasons why we are baptized.

Nephi taught: "I know that if ye shall follow the Son, with full purpose of heart, acting no hypocrisy and no deception before God, but with real intent, repenting of your sins, witnessing unto the Father that ye are willing to take upon you the name of Christ, by baptism - yea, by following your Lord and your Savior down into the water, according to his word, behold, then shall ye receive the Holy Ghost; yea, then cometh the baptism of fire and of the Holy Ghost; and then can ye speak with the tongue of angels, and shout praises unto the Holy One of Israel." (2 Nephi 31:13).

He added the testimony of the Father to his own words: "And I heard a voice from the Father, saying: Yea, the words of my Beloved are true and faithful. He that endureth to the end, the same shall be saved." (2 Nephi 31:15). It is not often in the scriptures that the solemn testimony of God the Father is recorded, but baptism is such an important ordinance of the Gospel and is so central to the Doctrine of Christ that it merits such attention. Just so, the same holy witness attended the baptism of Jesus at Jordan. (See Matthew 3:17).

The atoning blood of Jesus Christ cleanses, while the Holy Ghost purges the effects of sin. (See Moses 6:60). "For the gate by which ye should enter is repentance and baptism by water; and then cometh a remission of your sins by fire and by the Holy Ghost." This puts us on the "strait and narrow path that leads to eternal life." (2 Nephi 31:17-18).

Then, we must "press forward" with complete dedication and "steadfastness," or confidence and a firm determination in Christ, "having a perfect brightness of hope," or perfect faith, and charity, or "a love of God and of all men." If we do this, "feasting upon the word of Christ," or receiving strength and nourishment from the scriptures, and endure to the end in righteousness, we "shall have eternal life," which is the greatest gift that God can bestow. (2 Nephi 31:20). This is our on-going opportunity and responsibility.

Nephi stated this doctrine in simple language that is difficult to misinterpret. "This is the way," he said, "and there is none other way nor name given under heaven whereby (we) can be saved in the kingdom of God. And now, behold, this is the Doctrine of Christ, and the only and true doctrine of the Father, and of the Son, and of the Holy Ghost, which is one God, without end." (2 Nephi 31:21).

This doctrine becomes the Gospel of the Father as well as of the Son and the Holy Ghost, because these three distinct members of the Godhead are One, in complete unity, love, and purpose. As we focus on the ordinance of baptism, we can see how our Father, His Son, and the Holy Ghost work together to provide the opportunity for us to have immortality and eternal life. "For by the water ye keep the commandment; by the Spirit ye are justified, and by the blood ye are sanctified." (Moses 6:60).

Christ is the Author of Salvation (Hebrews 5:9), and the Finisher of our Faith, (Hebrews 12:2), but The Plan was introduced to His spirit children by Heavenly Father. (See 2 Nephi 9:13). By the spirit of revelation, the Holy Ghost testifies of Christ and of the Father's Plan. (D&C 8:2-3). Working in perfect harmony, They promote the doctrine of Christ with one shared goal: to bring us to the waters of baptism, to the very Portal of the Celestial Kingdom.

One Hundred and One Reasons Why We Are Baptized

1.

We are baptized in submission to the law of heaven.

Do you think baptism has always been performed in the Lord's own way?

Anciently, there was confusion concerning the proper administration of the ordinance. "And it came to pass, that Abram fell on his face, and called upon the name of the Lord. And God talked with him, saying, My people have gone astray from my precepts, and have not kept mine ordinances, which I gave unto their fathers. And they have not observed mine anointing, and the burial, or baptism wherewith I commanded them." (J.S.T. Genesis 17:3-5).

How do some people "wrest the scriptures" that relate to baptism? (D&C 10:63).

They "have turned from the commandment, and taken unto themselves the washing of children, and the blood of sprinkling; And have said that the blood of the righteous Abel was shed for sins; and have not known wherein they are accountable before me." (J.S.T. Genesis 17:6-7).

Do you think the Savior's Apostles administered baptism correctly?

As long as the Apostles walked the earth, there was no disputation regarding the ordinance of baptism. When they were martyred, however, and their priesthood authority died with them, confusion arose concerning the simplest policies, procedures, and doctrines of the kingdom, and there was no enlightened solution to the problem.

What happened when the priesthood authority of the Apostles died with them?

Apostasy resulted, requiring the direct latter-day intervention of Heavenly Father and His Son Jesus Christ. (See J.S.H. 1:16-20).

We are baptized as a witness that we are willing to follow in the footsteps of the Savior.

What does it mean to follow the Savior with full purpose of heart? (See Mosiah 7:33).

It means to act without hypocrisy or deception before God, but instead, "with real intent, repenting of (our) sins, witnessing unto the Father that (we) are willing to take upon (ourselves) the name of Christ, by baptism - yea, by following (our) Lord and (our) Savior down into the water." (2 Nephi 31:13).

Why doesn't The Book of Mormon make any special mention of the manner of baptism among the Nephites?

Baptism by immersion was the standard. For example, when John the Baptist went into the wilderness of Judea preaching repentance and baptism, his actions didn't arouse any curiosity among the people, as if he were introducing some new and strange doctrine. The Jews of that day understood it as an essential Gospel ordinance, and so it was. Even the "Jewish Encyclopedia" states: "John stood forth in the spirit of the prophets of old to preach his baptism of repentance symbolized by cleansing with water."

When was the ordinance of baptism first administered?

Baptism is an ordinance of great antiquity, requiring humility and obedience before God the Father. "The Lamb of God...fulfil(ed) all righteousness in being baptized by water." (2 Nephi 31:6). He was indeed baptized, for as Elder Howard W. Hunter declared: "Jesus entered into all the saving ordinances of the Melchizedek Priesthood," and baptism qualifies one to participate in these.

Where in the scriptures do we learn about Adam's baptism?

"Adam cried unto the Lord, and he was caught away by the Spirit of the Lord, and was carried down into the water, and was laid under the water, and was brought forth out of the water. And thus he was baptized, and the Spirit of God descended upon him, and thus he was born of the Spirit, and became quickened in the inner man." (Moses 6:65-66).

3.

We are baptized to demonstrate our obedience to the will of the Savior.

How did the voice of the Lord teach Nephi about the ordinance of baptism?

"Follow me," it urged, "and do the things which ye have seen me do...with full purpose of heart, acting no hypocrisy and no deception before God, but with real intent, repenting of your sins, witnessing unto the Father that ye are willing to take upon you the name of Christ by baptism." (2 Nephi 2:12-15).

How difficult is it to follow the commandment to be baptized?

When we are obedient, we will not recoil from the uncertainties of mortality. Joseph F. Smith declared: "We need not fear in our hearts when we are conscious of having lived up to the principles of truth and righteousness as God has required it at our hands, according to our best knowledge and understanding."

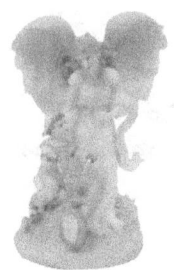

What happens when we surrender our will to the guidance of our Heavenly Father?

Parley P. Pratt declared: "I have received the Holy Anointing, and I can never rest until the last enemy is conquered, death destroyed, and truth reigns triumphant."

How can baptism influence our attitude about obedience?

After our baptism, we discover that obedience is no longer inconvenient, but has become our quest. In that moment, said Ezra Taft Benson, God endows us with power. When we are diligent in our obedience, our agency enjoys its greatest expression. This is one of the hardest things for the unconverted to understand.

We are baptized in similitude of the supreme act of humility by the Savior.

Why do you think the Savior chose to be baptized in the Jordan River?

He Who was our Exemplar descended beneath us all, both physically and symbolically, when He was baptized in Jordan, the lowest body of fresh water upon the face of the earth. In our own day, the meek shall inherit the earth, though "persecutions may rage, mobs may combine, armies may assemble, (and) calumny may defame." (Joseph Smith, in The Wentworth Letter, H.C. 4:540).

How can our baptism help us to feel better about ourselves?

Baptism is the temporal foreshadowing of a celestial celebration for which the preparations are already being made by a heavenly host. Baptism is both a commemoration and a commencement. It memorializes the completion of a long and arduous journey that began with a recognition of our dependence upon the Savior. It ends with the certification of our determination to serve God with full purpose of heart. At every baptism, the Holy Ghost is the life of the party, Who validates our commitment to see our work upon the earth through to its completion.

How is baptism related to the Atonement of Jesus Christ?

Because of the Atonement, we all have equal opportunity before the Lord. With free will comes the power to accept or reject the principles of the Plan that was created for our benefit before the world was made.

Why do you think 8 is described as the age of accountability? (See D&C 29:47).

Baptism at the age of eight captures the hearts of little children before they have been exposed to the cankering influence and corrosive elements of the world, before their hearts are set upon temporal things, and their spirituality has been so weakened that the things of God are no longer part of their daily experience. Better than the rest of us, little children have a capacity to "lay aside the things of this world, and seek for the things of a better." (D&C 25:10).

5.

We are baptized to "fulfill all righteousness." (Matthew 3:15).

How can envisioning our own baptism make us feel so good inside?

We turn our thoughts to the Savior, Whose teachings speak to our spirits. The Holy Ghost illuminates our minds, and when our eyes become single to the glory of God, we are filled with light. (See J.ST. Matthew 6:22). We enjoy a fluency, a familiarity, and an ease with the doctrines, and a comfort with the principles of The Plan that reveals vistas of eternal proportion. With our baptism, Heavenly Father certifies that the day will come that we will see Him, for He will unveil His face to us. But it will be in His own time, and in His own way, and according to His will. (See D&C 88:68).

Why do you think the Savior, Who was without sin, submitted to baptism?

The Lord was baptized as an example to us that we must obey every commandment and participate in every ordinance that God has decreed are necessary to attain eternal life. (See 2 Nephi 31:5).

How can parents encourage their children to be baptized?

The baptism of children who have arrived at the age of accountability is the culmination of a process begun much earlier, when their caregivers introduced them to the concepts pertaining to The Plan of Salvation, by preaching, teaching, and expounding upon the principles, and by then bringing them into focus with meaningful illustrations. Finally, their charges are introduced to instruction that expounds upon the principles, leading to an expansion of understanding. (See D&C 20:46-52).

What else can parents do to prepare their children for baptism?

The worth of principles is validated through personal witness or testimony. The desire to be baptized becomes the outward expression of a personal dedication to obedience. It is the public manifestation of the desire to have a private covenant relationship with God. It is the voluntary surrender of agency to a higher power, the subjugation of our will, to His will. It represents a promise and a covenant that young and impressionable minds can easily grasp.

We are baptized to receive a remission of our sins, if we have reached the age of accountability.

What has the Atonement of Jesus Christ got to do with baptism?

The atoning blood of Jesus Christ cleanses, while the Holy Ghost purges the effects of sin. (See Moses 6:60). "For the gate by which (we) should enter is repentance and baptism by water; and then cometh a remission of (our) sins by fire and by the Holy Ghost." This puts us on the "strait and narrow path that leads to eternal life." (2 Nephi 31:17-18).

Why do you think God has given us the commandment to be baptized?

We must be baptized for the remission of sins. The foundation principle upon which the ordinance is anchored is based upon an injunction found throughout the canon of scripture: "Repent, and be baptized every one of you in the name of Jesus Christ for the remission of sins." (Acts 2:38).

Who are the only perfect examples of those who are free from the stain of sin?

Jesus, together with little children, are cited in the scriptures as the only perfect examples. He said: "Ye must repent, and be baptized in my name, and become as a little child, or ye can in nowise inherit the kingdom of God." (3 Nephi 11:38).

What can happen to the innocence of children?

As William Wordsworth observed: "Heaven lies about us in our infancy. Shades of the prison house begin to close upon the growing boy. But he beholds the light and whence it flows; he sees it in his joy. The youth, who daily farther from the east must travel, still is nature's priest. And by the vision splendid, he is on his way attended. At length, the man perceives it die away, and fade into the light of common day."

7.

We are baptized to gain admission to the Lord's church, which is "the only true and living church upon the face of the whole earth" with which He is pleased. (D&C 1:31).

How is baptism Heavenly Father's formal invitation to come into the Savior's fold and to be called His people? (See Mosiah 18:8).

"All those who humble themselves before God, and desire to be baptized (who) have truly repented of all their sins...shall be received by baptism into his church." (D&C 20:37).

What other qualities must we have, before we are baptized?

In a beautiful admonition, Alma described the qualities that members strive for as they enter the waters of baptism. "Be humble," he said, "and be submissive and gentle; easy to be entreated; full of patience and long-suffering; being temperate in all things; being diligent in keeping the commandments of God at all times; asking for whatsoever things ye stand in need, both spiritual and temporal, always returning thanks unto God for whatsoever things ye do receive. And see that ye have faith, hope, and charity, and then will ye always abound in good works." (Alma 7:23-24).

How does baptism help to create a Zion society?

The characteristics of a Zion society are simply the result of a spiritual transformation in the lives of those who have been baptized and confirmed as members of the Church of Jesus Christ.

To whom is admission to the Lord's Church reserved?

Peter said: "Of a truth, I perceive that God is no respecter of persons: But in every nation, he that feareth him, and worketh righteousness, is accepted with him." (Acts 10:34-35). In particular, the Gentile nations of the earth are to receive the Gospel, and the elect among them are to be converted by the power of the Holy Ghost, to be carried along the path leading to baptism.

> We are baptized that we might
> experience sanctification through
> fire and the Holy Ghost.
> (See Mosiah 5:7).

What is one of the special responsibilities of the Holy Ghost?

It is to bear a sacred witness of the validity of every Gospel ordinance. Because there can be no greater witness, the Atonement is completed by the baptism of fire and the unimpeachable witness of the Holy Ghost. In baptism, Mercy satisfies Justice, and the penitent faithful receive a remission of sins in a symbolic rite of purification. (See 2 Nephi 31:17).

How is Heavenly Father a party to every Gospel covenant?

Those who make sacred promises with Him at the waters of baptism will be visited "with fire and with the Holy Ghost." (3 Nephi 11:36). Fire and smoke have always been symbolic of the presence of the Lord and of the glory of celestial realms. His Spirit is like a burning fire. In the language of Joseph Smith: "God Almighty Himself dwells in eternal fire. Our God is a consuming fire." (See Deuteronomy 4:24, & Hebrews 12:24).

Why must we be baptized before we can receive the gift of the Holy Ghost?

"Every individual that lives according to the laws that the Lord has given to His people, and has received the blessings that He has in store for the faithful, will be able to know the things of God from the things which are not of God, the light from the darkness, that which comes from heaven, and that which comes from somewhere else. This is the satisfaction and the consolation that the Latter-day Saints enjoy by living their religion. This is the knowledge which every one who thus lives possesses." (Brigham Young).

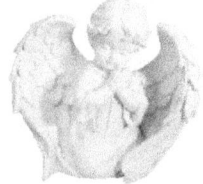

What kinds of worldly influences are constantly at work to drive away the Spirit?

Satan has focused significant energies and invested immense resources to neutralize the influence of the Holy Ghost. He works under the radar by creating economic burdens to get mothers out of the home and into the workplace. He employs political pressures under the guise of "equality" and "equal opportunity." Within the ivory towers of academia, he tutors the rising generation with carefully groomed mentors who rail against every proven principle.

We are baptized that we might be spiritually begotten of Christ.
(See Mosiah 5:7).

What was the experience of Joseph Smith following his own baptism?

He wrote: "Our minds being now enlightened, we began to have the scriptures laid open to our understandings, and the true meaning and intention of their more mysterious passages revealed unto us in a manner which we never could attain to previously, nor ever before had thought of." (J.S.H. 1:74).

What did Jesus teach Nicodemus about being "born again," (John 3:3) and about being "spiritually begotten?" (Mosiah 5:7).

We are taught that as we are immersed in the healing waters, we are born again. "Nicodemus saith unto him, How can a man be born when he is old? Can he enter the second time into his mother's womb, and be born? Jesus answered, Verily, verily, I say unto thee, Except a man be born of water and of the Spirit, he cannot enter into the kingdom of God." (John 3:4-4).

How does The Plan make it easier for us to be sensitive to the Spirit?

During the Creation, God made "the greater light to rule the day, and the lesser light to rule the night." (Genesis 1:16). It is illuminating to think of the greater light as the Holy Ghost, and the lesser light as the Light of Christ. The purpose of the lesser light would be to lead Heavenly Father's children to His doorstep, where the greater light of the Holy Ghost would be waiting to invite them, through the portal of baptism, to enjoy His grace.

How can baptism help us to edit the story of our lives?

When we are spiritually begotten of Christ, we are given the invitation to re-write the record of our lives. We cannot go back and start a new beginning, but we can begin now to make a new ending. Our lives can become fairytales that are waiting to be written.

> We are baptized that our hearts
> might be changed through faith
> on the name of Jesus Christ.
> (See Mosiah 5:7).

How is our desire to be baptized linked to faith?

Faith does not come without effort. It is a gift that must be earned. We are taught: "Behold, you have not understood; you have supposed that I would give it unto you, when you took no thought save it was to ask me. But, behold, I say unto you, that you must study it out in your mind." (D&C 9:7-8). "It is impossible to advance in the principles of truth, to increase in heavenly knowledge, except we exercise our reasoning faculties and exert ourselves." (Lorenzo Snow). We exercise our agency to increase in faith, but it is not free. It is purchased at a substantial price.

What blessings do we receive as our hearts are changed through faith?

"All saints who remember to keep and do these sayings, walking in obedience to the commandments, shall receive health in their navel and marrow to their bones; and shall find wisdom and great treasures of knowledge, even hidden treasures; and shall run and not be weary, and shall walk and not faint. And I, the Lord, give unto them a promise, that the destroying angel shall pass them by, as the children of Israel, and not slay them." (D&C 89:18-21).

How would you describe your faith in Christ?

It is not naiveté or gullibility, nor is it wishful thinking. It is more than confidence and greater than optimism. Faith and positive thinking go hand in hand, but faith is more than an attitude. Faith is not to receive a sign from heaven, because faith precedes the miracle. We have faith to believe what we do not see, but the reward of faith is to see what we believe.

How did you develop your faith?

During its genesis, it is necessary to take a few steps into the darkness. Then faith, the spiritual strong searchlight, will illuminate the way. Ultimately, our faith is confirmed by direct experience with the Spirit, in a validation that its Author and Finisher is God.

We are baptized that we might be born of Jesus Christ.
(See Mosiah 5:7).

Why would the prophets teach that it is necessary to be born again?

Birth is not a question of development or of maturation, but rather of generation. It is one of the most emotional, miraculous, and awe-inspiring events of mortality. Just so, the process of kindling our divine spark, of igniting the spirit lying dormant within us, of awakening our divine potential, and of nurturing the God in embryo that is present within each of us, is described as being "born again."

How can baptism help us to internalize eternal principles? (See Jeremiah 31:33).

The ordinance of baptism is of such power that it drives the law into our inward parts, so that it is written upon our hearts. A mighty change takes place as we experience the process of sanctification. When we are born again, the desired result of all Gospel-oriented teaching has been achieved, and we have no more disposition to do evil, but to do good continually. (See Mosiah 5:2).

For what purpose is the law driven into our inward parts? (See Jeremiah 31:33).

When the law is woven into the sinews of our souls, it becomes the very pattern upon which we trace our progress. The tapestry of our lives is "single to God, and the days will come that (we) shall see him; for he will unveil his face" unto us. (D&C 88:68).

How can baptism heal our spiritual blindness? (See John 9:39-41).

The key to our liberation from our bondage to sin, to our freedom to become, is an attitude adjustment that is reflected in our desire to be born again. To paraphrase Helen Keller, the real tragedy is not to be born without sight, but to live without vision.

We are baptized in a symbolic re-birth, as we pass through a tangible portal in the similitude of the grave.

What is the "similitude of the grave?" (D&C 128:13).

"Know ye not that, so many of us as were baptized into Jesus Christ were baptized into his death? Therefore, we are buried with him by baptism into death, that like as Christ was raised up from the dead by the glory of the Father, even so we also should walk in newness of life" through the process of being born again, symbolized by baptism by immersion. (Romans 6:3).

To what end are we re-born?

"For if we have been planted together in the likeness of his death, we shall be also in the likeness of his resurrection. Knowing this, that our old man is crucified with him, that the body of sin might be destroyed, that henceforth we should not serve sin." (Romans 6:5-6).

What did the Savior teach the Nephites about the symbolism of baptism?

Immersion in water is symbolic of the burial of Christ. (See 3 Nephi 11:23). Joseph Smith said the repentant are "baptized after the manner of his burial, being buried in the water in his name, and this according to the commandment which he has given - That by keeping the commandments they might be washed and cleansed from all their sins." (D&C 76:51-52). "Consequently, the baptismal font was instituted as a similitude of the grave." (D&C 128:13).

What was the instruction given by the Apostle Paul, that related to baptism?

Paul taught that being immersed in water and coming out again is symbolic of death and resurrection. He wrote: "For if we have been planted together in the likeness of his death, we shall be also in the likeness of his resurrection." (Romans 6:4).

13.

We are baptized in order to qualify for the blessings that are found in the other ordinances of the Gospel.

What has the Savior promised to give us when we are baptized?

He declared: "Whoso believeth in me, and is baptized...shall inherit the kingdom of God." (3 Nephi 11:33).

What blessings may we receive when we are baptized?

We "come out of the world, leaving the loneliness and estrangement of a fallen creation to enter the realm of divine experience. We forsake the orphanage of spiritual alienation, to be received into the family and household of the Lord Jesus Christ." (Doctrinal Commentary on The Book of Mormon," 4:202).

How does our baptism qualify us to call ourselves Christians? (See Acts 26:28).

"We leave the ranks of the nameless, and take upon ourselves the blessed name of Jesus Christ. We become Christians. Through our Master, we become, in time, joint heirs of all that the Father has." ("Doctrinal Commentary on The Book of Mormon" 4:202).

Are the guidelines for baptism subject to private interpretation? (See 2 Peter 1:20).

The ordinance of baptism has not been arbitrarily established, with corollaries, footnotes, or exceptions to the rule. The commandment to be baptized is not subject to appeal, amendment, or interpretation. The principle has a doctrinal foundation that is central to The Plan of Salvation, for it is the hinge upon which swings the gate leading to eternal life with Heavenly Father.

14.

> We are baptized that we might be better prepared
> to travel the established path that leads
> to the Celestial Kingdom of God.

How does baptism make it easier for us to return to our Heavenly Home?

We make a significant statement with our baptism of water. But with the baptism of fire and the Holy Ghost, God makes an unprecedented proclamation. The Spirit is our key to knowledge past, present, and future, and to truth that never has been revealed from the foundation of the world, but has been kept hid from the wise and prudent. These mysteries "shall be revealed unto babes and sucklings in this, the dispensation of the fulness of times." (D&C 128:18).

After our baptism, how does the path that leads back Home open up before us?

After baptism, we await the further light and knowledge the Lord has promised to send to us. "For God, who commanded the light to shine out of darkness, hath shined in our hearts, to give the light of the knowledge of the glory of God in the face of Jesus Christ." (2 Corinthians 4:6).

How does The Plan hold "the key to the mysteries of the kingdom?" (D&C 84:19).

Baptism open up windows of opportunity to better understand the principles of the Gospel, that are mysteries to those who have not spiritually prepared themselves for personal revelation from God. The Lord has assured us that we "shall know of a surety that these things are true, for from heaven will (He) declare it unto (us)." (D&C 5:12). When we are asked, as Antionah asked of Alma: "What does the scripture mean?" because of our baptism, we will know when and how to teach these principles that relate to doctrine. (Alma 12:21).

How is baptism our R.S.V.P. to God's invitation to join the fold?

Baptism is an R.S.V.P. that so delights God, that He causes it to catalyze our liberation from fear, doubt, apprehension of danger, the turmoil of the world, and the vagaries of men. It emancipates us from the self-limiting conditions that had heretofore blinded us to a larger view of life. It frees us to pay closer attention to celestial guideposts and principles. It invites us to experience more intense and reflective self-awareness, deeper and more abiding humility, reinvigorated confidence, and incomprehensibly more profound and enduring faith.

15.

We are baptized in the temporal expression of a spiritual reality.

How is baptism a "type?"

Baptism is symbolic; it has not only a present meaning, but also points to a future blessing or reality. Those who have moved beyond the age of accountability are buried in the cleansing water, to come forth in a newness of life, to be born again, that they might not suffer the second, or spiritual, death.

How are Gospel principles different from the shifting values of the world?

Gospel principles are truths that are eternally valid. Values are beliefs that are culturally or personally determined, and that may change with circumstances. Baptism is an ordinance that is the expression of a Gospel principle. The reason that a correct understanding of baptism is essential is that it is a foundation ordinance that lies at the very heart of the doctrine of the Gospel of Jesus Christ.

Why do you think Heavenly Father chose water as the medium to convey spiritual truth?

Water may be the most common substance in the universe, and immersion is something to which all of God's children can relate. Anciently, those who wrote the Dead Sea Scrolls described their own experience: "Our flesh is cleansed shining bright in the waters of purification, even in the waters of baptism."

How is baptism related to our adoption into the House of Israel?

Adoption grants us access to a privileged proximity to the priesthood. It exposes us to the New and Everlasting Covenant made anciently with our father Abraham. These are expressions that are related to both present and anticipated temporal and spiritual realities.

16.

> We are baptized that we might overcome
> spiritual death, and come into the
> presence of the Father, the Son,
> and the Holy Ghost.

Why do you think the baptismal prayer addresses Heavenly Father, as well as Jesus Christ, and the Holy Ghost?

As the officiant invokes their sacred names, all three members of the Godhead are invited to attend the baptismal service. The right arm is raised to the square in a symbolic gesture, as if it were reaching out to the delicious fruit of the tree of life. The sweet sensations of its taste are indelibly imprinted upon the minds of all who are present to witness the spiritual transformation to a god in embryo.

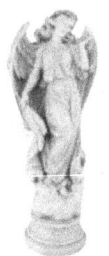

Why do you think Heavenly Father bore His testimony at the baptism of His Son?

It is not often in the scriptures that the solemn testimony of God the Father is recorded. Baptism is such an important ordinance of the Gospel and is so central to the Doctrine of Christ that it merited the attention of God's holy witness, that attended and sanctioned the baptism of Jesus at Jordan. (See Matthew 3:17).

How does the Light of Christ influence us to come to the waters of baptism?

Until we are baptized, we abide by the Light of Christ, and only receive a taste of the limitless power and intrinsic spiritual illumination that rests within the Godhead. Following our baptism, however, we are blessed with an awakening comprehension, and we begin to understand that our "Father, and the Son, and the Holy Ghost are one," and that they share a palpable divine power and authority that are directed to our benefit, in an infinite variety of ways. (3 Nephi 11:27).

Have you ever wondered how the Holy Ghost completes the "Holy Trinity?"

The Holy Ghost dazzles us with an endless reserve of revelation that provides illumination to every corner of our minds and our spirits. The promises proffered by the combined capacity of the intrinsic light possessed by the Holy Trinity, then, is beyond our comprehension.

17.

We are baptized in a palpable expression of the Doctrine of Christ.

Where in the scriptures has the Doctrine of Christ been most clearly articulated?

Simply stated, Nephi explained that this doctrine is that all who have faith in Jesus Christ and truly repent of their sins, entering into a baptismal covenant with Him, will receive the Holy Ghost, Who will then direct their way, showing them the things they must do to merit the grace of God and inherit salvation. (See 2 Nephi Chapter 31).

Whose doctrine is it that finds expression in the Gospel?

This doctrine is properly the Gospel of the Father as well as of the Son and the Holy Ghost, because these three distinct members of the Godhead are One, in complete unity, love, and purpose.

How does the Holy Ghost help us to recognize the Doctrine of Christ?

The ordinances of baptism and the receipt of the Holy Ghost, are the "fruit of the Spirit, (Galatians 5:22), that we receive when we have been taught the Doctrine of Christ. As Nephi explained: "If ye will enter in by the way…it will show unto you all things what ye should do. Behold, this is the doctrine of Christ" (2 Nephi 32:5-6).

How does baptism help us to maintain our focus on the Doctrine of Christ?

The ordinance of baptism helps us to appreciate how all three members of the Godhead work in our behalf to provide the blessing of immortality and eternal life. "For by the water (we) keep the commandment; by the Spirit (we) are justified, and by the blood (we) are sanctified." (Moses 6:60).

18.

We are baptized to facilitate the temporal implementation of The Plan of Salvation.
(See D&C 3:1).

Have you ever thought about how brilliantly The Plan of Salvation has been scripted?

The Plan of Salvation allows us to monitor our relationship with our Heavenly Father, as we prepare to be reunited with Him. It is founded upon the points of doctrine that focus on Salvation, and upon these elements hinges its correct understanding. The "Plan of Salvation," as it turns out, is a very good choice of words when describing the intimacy that our Heavenly Father desires to have with each of us.

For what purpose was The Plan of Salvation conceived?

The Plan of Salvation is a practical model that allows us to reconcile our place in the cosmos with eternity, by giving us down to earth instruction relating to our divine potential. It gives us the tools to work out our salvation before the Lord. (See Philippians 2:12).

How does The Plan help us to bridge the gap between mortality and eternity?

The Plan creates a link between the realities of our physical world and the promises of eternity, and seamlessly harmonizes the two in ways that provide us with practical tools we can use to hash out the details of our progression toward that "undiscovered country from whose bourn no traveler returns." (Shakespeare, "Hamlet").

How do the 7 "Rs" prepare us to meet our Heavenly Father?

The Atonement is the only reasonable alternative to an otherwise overwhelmingly negative influence competing for dominance in our lives. The only stipulation of the Atonement is that we go through the process of repentance wherein we Recognize our transgression, experience Remorse, Renounce the self-defeating behavior, Resolve to do better, make Restitution where possible, and then do our part to establish a Reconciliation with the Spirit, and ultimately Receive a Remission of sin through the grace of God our Redeemer.

19.

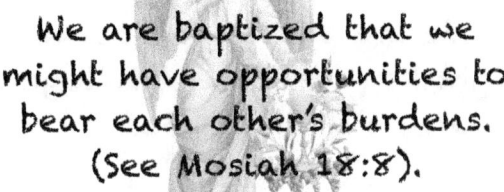

We are baptized that we might have opportunities to bear each other's burdens. (See Mosiah 18:8).

How can we help to bear each other's burdens?

Since Cain first made the inquiry, we have grappled with the question: "Am I my brother's keeper?" (Genesis 4:9). As true disciples, however, we engage in acts of quiet Christianity. "There are some people in this world," John Taylor declared, "who, if a man were poor or hungry, would say, let us pray for him. I would suggest a little different regimen for a person in this condition. Rather, take him a bag of flour and a little beef or pork. A few such comforts will do him more good than your prayers." (C.R., 10/1877).

How can we give more freely of ourselves?

When a child of God is down and out, an ounce of help is better than a pound of preaching. Socrates said, "Know thyself." Cicero urged, "Control Thyself." But the Gospel teaches that we must give of ourselves. (See 1 Timothy 4:15). We establish our commitment to actively embrace the demands of discipleship by following the example of the Master. After all, "are we not all beggars?" asked Benjamin. "Do we not all depend upon the same Being, even God, for all the substance which we have?" (Mosiah 4:19).

How can we help others without enabling them?

Helping hands are not synonymous with handouts and the sooner we recognize that we are on the "dole," the faster we can get off it. We may not be standing in line at soup kitchens, and we may not be receiving free turkey dinners at the Union Gospel Mission, but in whatever circumstances we find ourselves, we need "to stand independent above all other creatures." (D&C 78:14).

What should we do if we feel someone is not deserving of our help?

We cannot allow our prejudices to determine the depth of our compassion, or debate the merits of the petitions of the impoverished. We can learn from the example of the Sons of Mosiah, who ignored the outcries of those who characterized the Lamanites as "a stiffnecked people, whose hearts delight in the shedding of blood, whose days have been spent in the grossest iniquity, whose ways have been the ways of a transgressor from the beginning." (Alma 26:23-25).

20.

> We are baptized that we
> might be given the privilege to
> "mourn with those that mourn."
> (Mosiah 18:9).

How can we help to put smiles on the faces of those who mourn?

When we mourn with those who mourn, we smile with all our heart and with all our might. If we do nothing else, we can be the smile on the faces of those who mourn, or stand in need of comfort.

How can baptism help those who mourn to look at life with new eyes?

"If we looked at mortality as the whole of existence, then pain, sorrow, failure, and short life would be calamity. But if we look upon life as an eternal thing stretching far into the pre-mortal past and on into the eternal post-death future, then all that happens may be put in proper perspective." (Spencer W. Kimball, "Faith Precedes The Miracle," p. 103).

How difficult would it be to face life's hardships without the support of the Gospel?

Without the influence of the Savior, "we wait for light, but behold obscurity; for brightness, but we walk in darkness. We grope for the wall like the blind...as if we had no eyes: we stumble at noonday as in the night; we are in desolate places as dead men. We roar like bears, and mourn sore like doves: we look for judgment, but there is none; for salvation, but it is far off from us. For our transgressions are multiplied before (God), and our sins testify against us." (Isaiah 59:9-12).

How does knowing that we are the children of God help us to face adversity?

A light blazes from the Savior, that is reflected upon the shining waters of purification. It beckons us to dwell within the secure envelope of the word of God, Who is "a lamp unto (our) feet, and a light unto (our) path." (Psalms 119:105).

21.

> We are baptized that we might comfort those that stand in need of comfort."
> (Mosiah 18:9).

Why is "Comforter" an appropriate name for the Holy Ghost?

With our baptism comes "the remission of sins (which) bringeth meekness, and lowliness of heart; and because of meekness and lowliness of heart cometh the visitation of the Holy Ghost, which Comforter filleth with hope and perfect love, which love endureth by diligence unto prayer, until the end shall come, when all the saints shall dwell with God." (Moroni 8:26).

Why do you think we are asked to provide comfort to the downtrodden?

Baptism pushes us out of comfort zones that can be suffocating to our spirits. Our covenant of baptism is designed to make saints of sinners as it works on us; so much so that we begin to hate our former lives in the world, and strive to be better than we have ever been before, by finding ways to minister to the needs of others. (See John 12:25).

How does baptism help us to choose the harder right, instead of the easier wrong?

We must guard against languishing at the aid stations that are invitingly scattered throughout Babylon. These offer few comforts for those who should be pressing forward with a steadfastness in Christ. They provide little solace for those who struggle to watch their thoughts, words, and deeds. They tender no succor to those who strive, day by day, to keep the commandments, and they afford no consolation to those who endure to the end in righteousness.

How does baptism empower us to choose wisely?

We are free to choose how we will respond in any given situation. "Between stimulus and response, there is a space. Therein is our power to choose and therein lies our growth and our freedom. Forces beyond our control can take away everything we possess except one thing, our freedom to choose how we will respond to the situation." (Victor Frankel). It is within that space that we choose to "comfort those that stand in need of comfort."

We are baptized that we might have the courage "to stand as witnesses of God at all times and in all things, and in all places that (we) may be in." (Mosiah 18:9).

What is our responsibility to bear witness of the truth?

The Gentiles are to be converted by the power of the Holy Ghost. Peter, who first brought the Gospel to the Gentiles, wrote: On them "also was poured out the gift of the Holy Ghost." (Acts 10:45). This gift is sufficient to propel the elect of God along the path leading to eternal life.

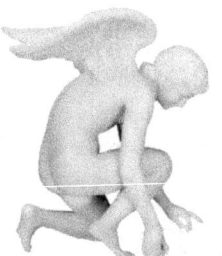

How seriously must we take our witness of Christ?

Our witness must be genuine; it must come from our hearts, as well as our heads. Our witness cannot ring hollow. Taking it lightly betrays an inner emptiness that cannot be satisfied with the poor imitations of the inner peace that could have been ours. Anything less than complete obedience to our baptismal covenant to witness for Christ will surely estrange us from the Spirit, until we are left with neither root nor branch.

How is our witness of Christ quickened, after our baptism?

We witness for Christ by our actions. Our righteous example may be the only "pamphlet" those who are not members of the Church ever "read."

Is it possible for all of Heavenly Father's children to be witnesses of Christ?

The Gospel envisions God's creations as "one great city, full of beloved ones, divine and human, by nature endeared to each other." (Epictetus). He is the Grand Architect of the design that establishes the brotherhood of man even as it confirms His fatherhood, so that "in him we live, and move, and have our being; as certain also of (our) own poets have said. For we are also his offspring." (Acts 17:28). Family ties that are forged in heaven and tempered in mortality create an unbreakable bond.

23.

> We are baptized that we might "be redeemed of God, and be numbered with those of the first resurrection, that (we might) have eternal life."
> (Mosiah 18:9).

Why do you think that so many people ignorantly worship an unknown god?

The Athenians were not so very different from many in our day. Paul observed of them that they were inclined to bow down before unknown gods, whom they ignorantly worshipped. (See Acts 17:23). We are baptized in the hope that we might stand independently in our witness of Jesus Christ, the true and living God.

How does our desire to be baptized stand in contrast to those who have adopted a lifestyle that falls short of obedience to true principles?

Baptism is the gold standard for those who have previously identified with the Pharisees or the Sadducees, with Buddha, Confucius, Guru Nanak, Zoroaster, or with gods of wood and stone. It supplants the monotheism of Islam and the Bahá'í, the pantheistic theology of Hinduism, Shintoism, and Taoism, secular humanism, irreligion, Catholicism and Eastern Orthodoxy. It trumps evangelical Christianity, fundamentalism, Protestantism, as well as the existential nihilism of the postmodern world.

After baptism, what takes place within our hearts?

We learn how to ask Heavenly Father to heal the damage that has been inflicted upon us because of weakness in our armor. We recognize our failures, accept responsibility for the consequences, and take steps to restore the integrity of our moral shields, with a renewed dedication to our covenants. We accept counsel and instruction from the Spirit, and we feel the power of the Savior's Atonement. This knowledge becomes the foundation of a heart-healthy lifestyle that becomes our norm.

Why is the desire for the world's goods so traumatizing?

The treasures of the earth are worthless counterfeits for the blessings that God has reserved for the faithful. Only undisciplined minds are swayed by the siren song so seductively sent by Satan, and only unprincipled character crumbles in the face of tantalizing and traumatizing telestial temptations.

> We are baptized as a witness that we
> have made a covenant to serve God
> "and keep his commandments, that
> he (might) pour out his Spirit
> more abundantly" upon us.
> (Mosiah 18:10).

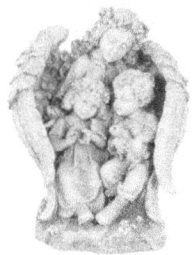

How does baptism help us to listen to spiritual promptings?

The Holy Ghost nudges us in the direction of our dreams. Ezra Taft Benson explained: "Answers to prayer come most often by a still voice and are discerned by our deepest, innermost feelings. We can know the will of God if we will take the time to pray, and to listen." We will be guided to Christ-like service if we put God first, and act upon the whisperings of the Spirit.

As we make covenants with God, how are we transformed?

We experience the thrill of being spiritually begotten of Him, and of having our hearts changed through faith on His name. He is ever before us, and without distraction our thoughts turn to Him. We feel His energy building within us until it lifts us to the zenith of experience where the lines distinguishing mortality from eternity blur, and we find ourselves consumed in a fire of everlasting burnings.

How do the whisperings of the Spirit encourage us to follow the Savior?

After the appearance of the resurrected Lord to the Apostles, Peter resumed his former occupation, and announced to the others, "I go a fishing." (John 21:3). But when the Savior appeared on the shore, and after He had instructed the Apostles, he said to Peter: "Follow me." (John 21:19). When the Savior figuratively appears beside the waters of baptism, we join Peter in the work of the ministry.

What does it mean to be "elect according to the foreknowledge of God?"

Following our baptism, a dawn of recognition comes to us, as we realize that we are the "elect according to the foreknowledge of God the Father, through sanctification of the Spirit, unto obedience and sprinkling of the blood of Jesus Christ." (1 Peter 1:2). We obtain "precious faith," and become partakers "of the divine nature." (2 Peter 1:1 & 4).

25.

> We are baptized that we might be
> given the tools we need to
> lengthen our stride.

After baptism, why does lengthening our stride sometimes cause discomfort?

The exertion stretches the limits of our stability in a violent confrontation between principles and values that tears at the fabric of the natural world. But in it, we find new spiritual strength. When we go the second mile by lengthening our stride, we burst free of the shackles that had limited the expression of our potential. We receive the "gift of spiritual independence that removes the veil of insensitivity to our destiny." (Richard L. Gunn).

Why would the Savior urge us to go the second mile? (See Matthew 5:41).

He knows that by doing so, we will capture an independence that can be exhilarating, because it is accompanied by the recognition of new-found and soul-expanding opportunities. It crystalizes within us the realization that we are spiritual beings having mortal experiences, and enables us with the sure knowledge that only the powers of heaven can countermand the dizzying inequities of life.

How are we fortified as we lengthen our stride?

As the process unfolds and we learn to balance our lives, our capacity to grow expands. We seize opportunities to be anxiously engaged in good causes. We think clearly, so that, on our own initiative, we can generate the power to avoid the conceptual cul-de-sacs, religious roundabouts, and doctrinal dead-ends that cause so many to lose their way.

How does lengthening our stride push us out of our comfort zones?

Each of us has 168 hours each week, much of it discretionary time to do with as we please. As few as three of these hours are spent in church. We need to ask ourselves: How many hours are wasted while "hanging out" in our comfort zones? How many hours are squandered watching television, playing video games, or on our computers or our mobile devices? How many hours do we devote to social media?

We are baptized that we might no more be "strangers and foreigners," but instead, "fellow citizens with the saints, and of the household of God."
(Ephesians 2:19).

How can we enjoy the companionship of the Saints.

Baptism amplifies the quiet spiritual stirrings that underlie our engagement with mortality. There are no social or genealogical qualifications that limit membership in the Church, or determine who may be the recipients of the blessings of the Gospel. Bringing "forth fruit meet for repentance" follows faith as the second principle and prerequisite that must be met before we may enjoy fellowship with the body of Christ. (Alma 13:13).

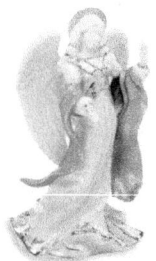

Why was Brigham Young concerned about the temporal welfare of the Saints?

He declared: "The worst fear that I have about this people is that they will get rich in this country, forget God and his people, wax fat, and kick themselves out of the church and go to hell. This people will stand mobbing, robbing, poverty, and all manner of persecution, and be true. But my greater fear for them is that they cannot stand wealth; and yet they have to be tried with riches, for they will become the richest people on this earth."

Why is it important to maintain associations with the Saints?

President Young said that Utah would become the crossroads of the west, "the great highway of the nations. Kings and emperors and the noble and wise of the earth will visit us here, while the wicked and ungodly will envy us our comfortable homes and possessions."

How is fellowship with the Saints a positive influence?

As we adopt the life-style of the Latter-day Saints, our proper prior priesthood preparation will prevent poor performance. It will nudge us off our complacency plateaus, away from the trendy cafés situated along the broad avenues of Idumea, and transport us, as on the wings of eagles, beyond the threshold of our self-imposed limitations, out to the edge of eternity, where "forever" will breathtakingly stand revealed before us.

27.

We are baptized that we might join the ranks of member missionaries.

Why did Paul say that we need not be embarrassed by the Gospel of Jesus Christ?

Those who are baptized are "not ashamed of the gospel of Christ, for it is the power of God unto salvation to every one that believeth." (Romans 1:16).

Who are the "elect according to the foreknowledge of God?" (1 Peter 1:2).

The elect among the Gentile nations of the earth are those who are most easily converted by the power of the Holy Ghost. Peter, who first brought the Gospel to the Gentiles, wrote: On them "also was poured out the gift of the Holy Ghost." (Acts 10:45). These gifts of the Spirit are sufficient to carry all of God's children along the path leading to eternal life.

Who, among all of Heavenly Father's children, are candidates for baptism?

Baptism permits us to see beyond the deserts of life. It transports us to the invisible summit of our imagination, even to the abode of the Gods, where the hint of a celestial breeze cools our cheeks. Heavenly Father has chosen us as His people, and He personally influences our destiny with a divine design. We live within His embrace, enjoying a security that others do not know. The baptism of fire and the Holy Ghost instills within us a desire to share our experience, that all might make a similar journey to Christ.

After we are baptized, how can we be good missionaries?

We can be valiant in the testimony of Jesus, and continue to make our offerings on the altar of faith. We can "take the Lord's side on every issue. We can think what He thinks, believe what He believes, say what He would say, and do what He would do." (Bruce R. McConkie).

We are baptized that we might continue "steadfastly in the apostles' doctrine and fellowship, and in breaking of bread, and in prayers."
(Acts 2:41-42).

What does it mean to be "firm and steadfast in the faith?" (Helaman 15:8).

Baptism allows us to "press forward" with complete dedication and with "steadfastness," or with confidence and a firm determination in Christ, "having a perfect brightness of hope," or perfect faith, and charity, or "a love of God and of all men." If we do this, "feasting upon the word of Christ," by receiving strength and nourishment from the scriptures, and if we endure to the end, not in wickedness, but in righteousness, we "shall have eternal life," which is the greatest gift that God can bestow. (2 Nephi 31:20).

What qualities must we develop if we are to provide Gospel instruction to others?

We must have hearts that have become the receptacles of true and virtuous principles upon which we may draw in times of need, bowels that are moved to compassion for those who are struggling with misfortune, hands that have been taught to lift those who are in need of support, and feet that have been conditioned to carry us to those who are imprisoned by poor choices, bad habits, or unfortunate circumstances.

Who are ministering angels?

These are heavenly messengers who are nursemaids to those with tender testimonies. They use their power as a resource to reach out and caress those among us who are poor in spirit. From time to time, we all feel their influence, for we have been assisted by acts of providence, are the beneficiaries of divine intervention, have been touched by angels, moved to compassion, or have been otherwise blessed to "walk in the light of the Lord." (Isaiah 2:5).

After baptism, how are we prompted by the Spirit?

Guidance in the form of spiritual promptings and impressions are more common that many would suspect. Powerful intuitive communicators strongly influence us to move in the direction of our dreams, toward a greater appreciation of the majesty and power of our Creator. Truly, He "is no respecter of persons" Who causes the sun to shine on the wicked, as well as on the just. (Acts 10:34, see Matthew 28:4).

29.

We are baptized that we might be clothed with
spiritual chain-mail, as protection against
the fiery darts of the adversary.
(See 1 Nephi 15:24).

How can Heavenly Father help us to resist Satan's temptations?

Baptism can replenish the power fueling our actions, giving our sight infinite perspective in the flow of a pulsing stream of inspiration that has no temporal or spatial boundary. As we are swept up by quickening currents into the direct experience of a holy communion with God, Satan's enticements lose their appeal as they fade in the brilliant light of day.

How can baptism by immersion extinguish the fiery darts of the adversary?

Although telestial turf is Satan's home ground, and the quicksand of secular humanism and other false ideologies lies ready to suck the unwary into the underworld of the adversary, "no power on earth or hell can overthrow or defeat that which God has decreed. Every plan of the adversary will fail, for the Lord knows the secret thoughts of men, and sees the future with a vision clear and perfect, even as though it were in the past." (Joseph Fielding Smith, Jr.).

How can we look past the temptations of the world?

Baptism encourages us to turn our thoughts to heaven, and although they will always be higher than ours, His thoughts will somehow have become our thoughts, and His ways our ways. (See Isaiah 55:8-9). We will be mesmerized by His work and His glory, and our baptism will nudge us ever closer to the realization that "the universe is a machine for the making of gods." (Henri Bergson).

How are free will, opposition, and baptism related?

Our baptism make a resounding statement that we have been born of God, have received His image in our countenances, and that we have experienced a mighty change in our hearts. (See Alma 5:14 & 26). Only then, through saving faith, will we be prepared to appropriately exercise our agency to decisively deal with the devil, as well as with the temporal trials that are a necessary element of The Plan of Salvation.

We are baptized that we might be released from bondage to sin.
(See D&C 84:49).

How can the Savior help us to free ourselves from the stain of sin?

As Benjamin so clearly taught: "Under this head ye are made free, and there is no other head whereby ye can be made free. There is no other name given whereby salvation cometh; therefore, I would that ye should take upon you the name of Christ, all you that have entered into the covenant with God that ye should be obedient unto the end of your lives." (Mosiah 5:8).

How do you feel about having prophets to whom we can turn for counsel?

From the foundation of the world, the Lord's servants have clarified again and again the first principles and ordinances of the Gospel Plan. Both the scriptures and the spoken word validate that "the Lord God will do nothing, but he revealeth his secret" unto His special witnesses. (Amos 2:7).

When we are baptized, Whose name do we take upon ourselves?

"And it shall come to pass that whosoever doeth this shall be found at the right hand of God, for he shall know the name by which he is called; for he shall be called by the name of Christ. And now it shall come to pass, that whosoever shall not take upon him the name of Christ must be called by some other name; therefore, he findeth himself on the left hand of God." (Mosiah 5:9-10).

How can we hope to effectively deal with the opposition in our lives?

Opposition is necessary for The Plan to function, and it makes baptism essential. Without it, we must remain in bondage to sin, for we all lack the spiritual horsepower to save ourselves. If we try to go it alone, we will suffer from a dearth of traction. We will be unable to generate spontaneity. Our lack of energy to engage enthusiasm will be noticeable, our incapacity to spark vitality will be evident, and our failure to candidly acknowledge the powerful relationship that can exist between ourselves and God will be clear. Truly, we need God every hour during our journey through life.

We are baptized that we might participate in the foundation ordinance of The Plan of Salvation.

What are days of probation?

Baptism helps to make our mission in mortality a time of testing, or of putting to the proof our declared values.

Why has baptism been likened to being reborn? (See John 3:3).

C.S. Lewis famously observed: "We can't go back and change the beginning, but we can start where we are and change the ending." Our re-birth frees us from the stain of sin that has been accumulating since the age of accountability. "Inasmuch as ye were born into the world by water, and blood, and the spirit, which I have made, and so became of dust a living soul, even so ye must be born again into the kingdom of heaven, of water, and of the Spirit, and be cleansed by blood, even the blood of mine Only Begotten." (Moses 6:59).

Why is baptism an essential element in the learning laboratory of life?

Experience is the active ingredient of a fertile matrix meticulously prepared by our Heavenly Father as the personalized petri dish that is best suited to our individual circumstances. This rich culture medium becomes just the agar we need in order to nurture our metamorphosis, as we are transformed into the full stature of our spirits. The infusion of a heavenly element readies us to receive with equanimity whatever might come during an incubation process that was initiated by divine design to be equally challenging and rewarding.

How can we make our baptismal covenant more meaningful?

The basic objectives of The Plan of Happiness are to keep the Savior in our thoughts, to encourage a daily atmosphere of reflection, to harmonize our behavior with His charitable example, to initiate positive change, and to maintain an eternal perspective.

> We are baptized by immersion in water, that we
> might feel not only the spiritual significance,
> but also the physical intensity, of the
> covenant we make with our
> Heavenly Father.

How can we join heavenly choirs to reach out and touch the face of God?

We can sing the songs of Zion that inspire, motivate, comfort, and strengthen us, while calming our troubled souls. Music and worship are elements of a unified whole. The instruments utilized, the way they are played, the volume and tempo, the lyrics if a vocal, the accompaniment, the attire and attitude of the performers, and the atmosphere in which the music is presented significantly influence our capacity for worship.

How can baptism help us to enjoy personal experiences with the Savior?

Our baptism becomes a complete submersion within the tangible element of Spirit. Skin is our largest organ system, wrapping us within two square meters of integumentary protection from the temporal elements. Because water is the "universal solvent," baptism by immersion becomes the perfect vehicle to penetrate its every pore, to both figuratively and literally dissolve away the inevitable detritus of organic, or telestial, waste, the caustic accretions of iniquity, and the corrosive scum lines of sin.

What might we want to record in our journals about how we felt at our baptisms?

Perhaps we can testify that "all the petty trials, sorrows, and sufferings of this life have faded away as temporary, harmless visions seen in a dream." (David O. McKay). Others will witness that our reverence for the Savior has been elevated to a category all by itself, where it can never legitimately fall under the scrutiny of a critical eye, be subjected to unrighteous judgment, or find itself compromised by association with the profane. Baptism sets the bar so high that, when the line is crossed by those who find fault with the Author of Salvation, their guilt will be immediately and incontrovertibly established, and the consequences of their actions sealed.

How can we tingle with the consciousness of our kinship with the infinite?

Boyd K Packer said that God will never take by force what He will accept when freely given. "And he will then return to you freedom that you can hardly dream of; the freedom to feel and to know, to do and to be. Strangely enough, the key to freedom is obedience." The secret to citizenship in Zion lies within an attitude adjustment reflected in our desire to be born again. Once more, we are reminded of the sagacity of Helen Keller, who said that the real tragedy in life is not those who are born without sight, but those who do not have vision.

33.

We are baptized as Jesus Christ invites us, by name, to become His disciples.

Is it possible that Jesus Christ knows each of us?

The words of the ordinance confirm that the Savior knows us by name, and takes the time to witness our baptism, that He might personally welcome us into His fold.

How is the covenant of baptism a two-way promise?

When we are baptized, we make covenants with our Heavenly Father to come into the fold of the Good Shepherd, to bear each other's burdens, to stand as witnesses of His Only Begotten Son at all times and in all places, and to serve Him and keep His commandments.

What does our Heavenly Father promise, in return?

In turn, He promises to forgive our sins, pour out His Spirit more abundantly upon us, give us daily guidance, allow us to come forth in the First Resurrection, and reward us with eternal life.

What does it mean to have His Spirit to be with us?

It means that we might feel the gentle caress of the hands of the Master Potter, as He turn our lives with the hand of time. It means that we have given Him permission, as the Artisan of our destiny, to mold us and shape us. (See Jeremiah 18:6). It means that we are the clay, and He is our potter; and we are the work of His hand. (See Isaiah 64:8). It means that as our thoughts turn to the Savior, we remain impressionable and pliable to His influence.

34.

We are baptized in a dramatic validation of the influence of the Light of Christ, and of the power of the Holy Ghost.

How does the Spirit inspire us? (See D&C 121:26).

The Holy Ghost works on our conscience, using the principles of The Plan to gently shepherd us to the covenants of the temple. "For behold, thus saith the Lord God: I will give unto the children of men line upon line, precept upon precept, here a little and there a little; and blessed are those who hearken unto my precepts, and lend an ear unto my counsel, for they shall learn wisdom; for unto him that receiveth I will give more." (2 Nephi 28:30).

For how long will the Holy Ghost strive with us?

"Till we all come in the unity of the faith, and of the knowledge of the Son of God, unto a perfect man, unto the measure of the stature of the fulness of Christ." (Ephesians 4:13).

How does the Light of Christ lead us to the Holy Ghost?

It animates our lives with energy. It proceeds from His throne as a powerful influence for good that grooms us to receive the Holy Ghost. It is a gift that miraculously multiplies even as it divides within a universe populated with countless individuals whose actions are governed by free will. It is given that we "may act in doctrine and principle pertaining to futurity, according to the moral agency" with which we have been amply endowed. (D&C 101:78).

How can the Light of Christ protect us from the influence of the adversary?

The Light of Christ has been benevolently bestowed upon all of us by One Whom, we can be sure, "is no respecter of persons." (Acts 10:34). The Light of Christ stimulates soul-sweat as it works on our conscience, our sense of duty, and our scruples, in such a way that we can meet the challenges of the relentless opposition in all things that has been integrated into The Plan. (See 2 Nephi 2:11).

35.

We are baptized to affirm the innocence of little children.

How can little children be saved from the foundation of the world? (See D&C 137:10).

It was an integral element of The Plan of Salvation, ordained in the Grand Council in Heaven before the world was, that little children who died before the age of accountability would be saved in the Celestial Kingdom by the power of the Atonement. "If not so, God is a partial God, and also a changeable God, and a respecter of persons; for how many little children have died without baptism!" (Moroni 8:12).

Why is the practice of infant baptism heretical?

It denies that Jesus Christ atoned for the "original sin" of Adam, and ignores the principle of individual accountability. It demands that little children who die without baptism cannot enter heaven. But the Atonement did redeem them from the Fall. They are capable of actions that are inconsistent with obedience to Gospel principles, but they are not counted against them as sins. Little children are not culpable.

What did Moroni have to say about baptism and accountability?

He wrote: "This thing shall ye teach - repentance and baptism unto those who are accountable and capable of committing sin; yea, teach parents that they must repent and be baptized, and humble themselves as their little children, and they shall all be saved with their little children." (Moroni 8:10).

How did Moroni link accountability to the baptism of little children?

He declared: "Little children need no repentance, neither baptism. Behold, baptism is unto repentance to the fulfilling the commandments unto the remission of sins. But little children are alive in Christ, even from the foundation of the world." (Moroni 8:11-12).

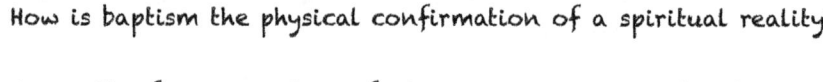

We are baptized that we might experience spiritual delight, without the rush of sensory overstimulation that is prevalent in our technological world.

How does baptism date back to an earlier time, when the pace of life was less hectic?

Baptism permits us to step back from the world to "caress the tender chords of human associations, of gratitude, loyalty, and appreciation, of selflessness, helpfulness and forgiveness, of friendship, love, and compassion." These are qualities that are most easily appreciated when we are far from the madding crowd.

How does baptism invite us to stay in touch with our five physical senses, while enhancing contact with our spiritual sixth sense?

It invites us to sense the world about us, "to smell its fragrance, hear its sounds, glimpse its form and colors, and warm our souls in the glow of human associations; to feel an upward reach when made suddenly aware of a truth, a beauty, or a goodness above and beyond our own attainment." (P.A. Anderson).

How is baptism the physical confirmation of a spiritual reality?

Our path of progress to perfection is a process, and not a point. We do not need to be the stars of the show. We do not need top billing to fulfill our dreams. We do not seek to garner a People's Choice Award. Rather than becoming the objects of attention of an adoring paparazzi, we foresee ourselves being enveloped in a dazzling cloud of divinely directed diamond dust that glitters with thousands of points of light. We become participants in daily dramas that far surpass the pomp and circumstance of any "American Idol" production.

How do the Light of Christ and the Holy Ghost work together to provide unmatched sensory stimulation?

As fire in the sky, the air in the theater of life is charged with an electricity that is generated by the inevitable merger of the universal encouragement of the Light of Christ with the pointed and providential guidance provided by the Holy Ghost. When these influences streak in tandem across the heavens, their trajectories coalesce to trace a flaming trail that sparkles over a vast cosmic ocean that is alive with energy. Over the ebb and flow of its tide, an effectual bridge of understanding is created, that is buttressed by the cohesive influence of the mighty foundation of faith.

37.

> We are baptized "for the perfecting of the saints, for the work of the ministry, (and) for the edifying of the body of Christ."
> (Ephesians 4:12).

What is the three-fold mission of the Church?

Paul would be in complete agreement with the mission of The Church of Jesus Christ of Latter-day Saints, which is to minister to others by preaching the Gospel, perfecting the Saints, and redeeming the dead.

What did Paul mean by the term: "the body of Christ?"

There is strength in numbers. Therefore, in the wisdom of God, His covenant children gather together in wards and stakes, that they might be mutually edified. They are a lot like snowflakes, that are one of nature's most fragile creations. Although delicate in structure, look at what they can do when they stick together.

What does it mean to edify the body of Christ?

The sturdiest plants that bear the best fruit are those that have deep roots in good, rich, nurturing soil. So, to edify the body of Christ, we must surround ourselves with the best that can be provided in music and art, conversation, example, decency, virtue, and honor. Then, with the members of the Church, we will grow freely, even as we send down taproots in Gospel soil to secure our solid footing.

How can those who have been baptized help to edify the body of Christ?

That the whole may be kept in perfect working order, and so that all those within the fold may expand their capabilities to the level of their potential, the Church "hath need of every member." (D&C 84:110).

38.

> We are baptized that we might "all come in the unity of the faith, and of the knowledge of the Son of God...unto the measure of the stature of the fulness of Christ."
> (Ephesians 4:13).

Why is it important for members of the Church to be unified in their faith?

Those who approach the fulness of the stature of Christ, are as coast redwood trees, that are among the largest living things. The tallest trees reach heights of over 360 feet, weighs hundreds of tons, and have been living for well over 2,000 years.

Why is unity in the faith critical to our survival?

Curiously, while most other trees of massive size have deep roots to support their great weight, the root system of the redwood is very shallow. The key to its survival is the intertwining of the roots of one tree with those of several of its neighbors. Redwoods live in groves; they cannot stand alone. Interdependence is critical to the stability and longevity of each individual tree.

How can baptism help us to become perfect in Christ? (See Moroni 10:32).

Baptism helps us to get off religious roundabouts, doctrinal dilemmas, and conceptual cul-de-sacs. We come unto Christ, and are perfected in him, as we deny ourselves of all ungodliness. If we do so, and "love God with all (our) might, mind and strength, then is his grace sufficient for (us), that by his grace (we) may be perfect in Christ." (Moroni 10:32).

What happens to us as we mature in the Gospel?

We become the sons and daughters of God, even one in our Savior Jesus Christ, as He is one in the Father, and the Father one in Him. (See D&C 35:2). Curiously, we retain our distinct individuality as we become unified in every other way.

39.

We are baptized "that we henceforth be no
more children, tossed to and fro."
(Ephesians 4:14).

How does baptism help us to face adversity?

Baptism helps us to be patient in our afflictions, for we shall have many. Knowing that the Lord is with us until the end of our days helps us to endure our trials and tribulations, even when they are undeserved, or when we do not understand why we have them. (See D&C 24:8).

How does our baptism help us to strengthen our relationship with Jesus Christ?

Because of our baptismal covenant, we will never be left to fight our battles alone. Baptism establishes a relationship with the Lord that invites Him to stand with us, to weigh in on our side of the scale, even as the counterfeit coin of Satan's spurious currency clatters down in a cacophony of confusion on the other side of the scale.

How should we interact with those who do not understand the principles of the Gospel?

As we interact with those who are struggling to feel even the influence of the Light of Christ, we must not pretend to know everything. We need to recognize when we are "speed listening," or forming a retort in our mind, when we should instead be listening attentively. We need to resist the temptation to treat every conversation as a debate. We need to ponder Isaiah's inspired counsel: "Come now, and let us reason together." (Isaiah 1:18).

What can we do when our friends are confused about the doctrine of baptism?

We should pose questions that lead to understanding, by frequently rehearsing the three magic words: "Tell me more." We should attentively listen for emotion, and always ask respectful questions. We need to discipline ourselves to pause before offering responses, and to ask ourselves: "How are our views similar?" and "Where is our common ground?"

> We are baptized that we might speak
> "the truth in love, (and) grow up
> into him in all things, which
> is the head, even Christ."
> (Ephesians 4:15).

How is it easier to "speak the truth in love" after our baptism?

Robert D. Hales said: "For the most part, conversion happens over a period of time as study, prayer, experience, and faith help us to grow in our testimony and conversion." (C.R., 4/1997). The fruits of faith come more easily to prepared minds; and nothing prepares us better than baptism!

How can baptism help us to "grow up into him in all things?"

Our baptism gives us the capacity to squarely face even our most stubborn challenges. It helps us to be unified with the Saints, even as we celebrate our individuality and diversity. It nurtures us to move from dependence, through independence, and finally to the mature state of interdependence. It gives us the tools to enjoy unity and conformity without sacrificing what has made each of us unique.

Can the Savior be our Head, if we are unwilling to submit to baptism?

The truth be told, many of our friends are very close to becoming members of the Church. If they would just change one or two behaviors or beliefs, they would be spot-on. Here's a radical thought, though. What if, instead, we changed just one or two of our behaviors, or viewed our neighbors' beliefs in a more tolerant light? Such an attitude adjustment could become a powerful tool of conversion.

How does baptism make it easier to speak the truth? (See Alma 60:23).

Worship is more than a repetitive exercise to be performed only by the numbers. Glad tidings elevate it to something more dynamic than the simple mechanical observance of a multiplicity of ceremonial rules. The Good News generates a groundswell of emotion that lifts us heavenward. Publishing peace is the daily antidote to our tendency toward pride, selfishness, and self-reliance. Put it all together, and witnessing for Christ helps us to create feeling, capture emotion, contour attitude, crystallize thought, congeal passion, compartmentalize action, and convey sentiments that lead to our spiritual revitalization.

41.

> We are baptized "unto the confounding of false doctrines and laying down of contentions."
> (2 Nephi 3:12).

How does baptism prepare us to confound false doctrines?

Baptism blesses us with a hope in Christ. It recalibrates our internal attitude control, quickens our desire to press forward, and encourages us to be righteous in the face of obstacles. Ultimately, baptism blesses us with the healing power of the Atonement and the grace of God when we fall short of our expectations.

How can we deal with the laying down of contention?

Baptism gives our spiritual muscles pliancy and flexibility, that there might be room for the companionship of the Holy Ghost, "which maketh manifest unto the children of men, according to their faith." (Jarom 1:4). We will always be subject to the effects of adversity and opposition, but without the therapeutic benefits of baptism, we may needlessly suffer from a stiff neck that prevents us from looking up to Heavenly Father for guidance, over to priesthood leaders for counsel, around to seek out those in need, and down in an attitude of humility.

How can baptism help us to be more patient as we face our adversaries?

There are 59 references to patience in the scriptures, including: "Bear with patience thine afflictions." (Alma 26:27). But we do not do so passively, as we would if we were biding our time at a traffic light. Instead, we are anxious, and the Lord engages the time while we are waiting upon Him to infuse us with strength, that we might mount up as with the wings of eagles. Permeated with His energy, we run without becoming weary, and we walk without fainting. (See Isaiah 40:31). Our patience, as it turns out, is not about how long we can wait, or about how we endure waiting, but about how we submit to the Lord while we are waiting, that He might mold and shape us.

Why is baptism as important a principle today as it has ever been in the past?

The Last Days mirror those of Mormon, who wrote that "there were sorceries, and witchcrafts, and magics, and the power of the evil one was wrought upon all the face of the land" because of the lack of faith of the people. (Mormon 1:19). Baptism is the spiritual equivalent of carbohydrate-loading before beginning a marathon. "The race is not to the swift, nor the battle to the strong," but to those who humble themselves before God and submit to His will. (Ecclesiastes 9:11).

> We are baptized that the light of our lives
> might grow "brighter and brighter
> until the perfect day."
> (D&C 50:24).

What is the light of our lives? (See Mosiah 27:29).

"The spirit of man is the candle of the Lord." (Proverbs 20:27). When they come into the world, every child of God has a full measure of light that represents the purity of the Spirit. Then, life becomes a process of detraction, in the sense that intrinsic light is lost as the children of men succumb to worldly cares. The Judgment may simply involve a measurement of the number of foot-candles of light remaining, that we bring to God's pleasing Bar. (See Moroni 10:34).

When we left heaven to come to earth, do you think we were full of light?

"Our birth, wrote Wordsworth, may be only "a sleep and a forgetting." Perhaps "the soul that rises with us, our life's star, hath had elsewhere its setting, and cometh from afar." If so, then "not in entire forgetfulness, and not in utter nakedness, but trailing clouds of glory do we come, from God, who is our Home."

How can we protect our light from the encroachment of darkness?

Politically correct tolerance embraces all sorts of deviant behavior. Flim flam artists adroitly fleece us of our very identity as children of God, and most of the time, we are not even aware that the theft is taking place. "Vice is a monster of such frightful mien, as to be hated needs but to be seen. Yet seen too oft, familiar with her face, we first endure, then pity, then embrace." (Alexander Pope). We have come full circle, from Eve's temptation in the Garden. Just as she was beguiled by the serpent, today we are mesmerized by tinkling cymbals and sounding brass. (See 1 Corinthians 13:1).

How can our baptism help us to be drawn to the light?

With baptism, there comes a familiarity with principles that stands in sharp contrast to the values of society that are continually morphed by the shifting sands of cultural expediency. The covenants we make at baptism protect us from these constantly mutating tenets, and provide a stable moral basis during our development into the full stature of our spirits.

We are baptized that the earth might "be full
of the knowledge of the Lord, as
the waters cover the sea."
(Isaiah 11:9).

Why is our participation in The Plan of Happiness important?

Our baptism leaves the world a better place than when we found it. When we pass beyond the veil, we will leave with our loved ones legacies of both tangible and intangible remembrances. We will leave them with our testimonies. We will leave them with shared gratitude for the privilege and blessing to have been knit together in a family that has become a basic building block of Heavenly Father's great Plan of Happiness.

How can the baptism of just one person make a positive difference in the world?

Our children are the nobility of heaven, a chosen generation with a divine destiny. We make whatever sacrifices are necessary to insure their continuing success. They come to us from their heavenly home "like gentle rain through darkened skies, with glory trailing from their feet as they go, and endless promise in their eyes." While under our care, they grow tall and strong, "like silver trees against the storm; who will not bend with the wind or the change, but stand to fight the world alone." (Doug Stewart).

How does baptism help us to trace our royal lineage, and teach us who we really are?

Baptism welcomes us to the ranks of "the few, the warriors saved for Saturday, who come the last day of the world. We are they, of Saturday. We are the strong, the warriors rising in our might to win the battle raging in the hearts of men, on Saturday. We are strangers from a realm of light, who have forgotten all - the memory of our former life and the purpose of our call. And so, we must learn why we're here, and who we really are." (Doug Stewart).

How can our obedience help to increase knowledge upon the earth?

Because the knowledge of the Lord will cover the earth, we need to plan our work and work His Plan. Its principles may be thought of as His blueprint that will transform His vision into our reality. The Plan defines the expenditure of faith that will be required to meet our challenges. Church organization provides clarity that facilitates the construction of a fitly framed building destined to grow "unto an holy temple for a habitation of God through the Spirit." (Ephesians 2:20-22).

44.

> We are baptized to capture the promise
> of "the peace of God, which
> passeth all understanding."
> (Philippians 4:7).

How can baptism define the pathway to peace?

Eight year olds who are baptized are so recently removed from the stability and certainty of the eternal world, that they are often impatient to recapture the peaceful security and quiet serenity of the more relaxed, familiar, and predictable spiritual environment to which they had become accustomed. Their baptism gives them the opportunity to literally have the best of both worlds; to live on earth, but still enjoy a heavenly peace that surpasses understanding.

How can we find peace in the world today?

The innocence of children who are about to be baptized makes us optimistic that peace is within our reach. When we become as little children, "submissive, meek, humble, patient, (and) full of love," the enticings of the Holy Spirit help us to put off natural tendencies and to become saints through the Atonement of Jesus Christ. (Mosiah 3:19).

How does the world's concept of peace differ from that to which baptism invites us?

The world's definition of peace is remarkably superficial: often-times peace is only equated with the lack of bloodshed or active combatants. The Lord's definition is quite different. "His peace is not the peace of the world of ease, of luxury, idleness, absence of turmoil and strife, but the peace born of the righteous life, the peace that lifts the soul, that day by day brings us closer to the home of Eternal Peace, the dwelling place of our Father." (J. Reuben Clark, Jr.).

Without baptism, can we ever truly be at peace?

Until we acknowledge the power of God, there will be no-one to whom we can turn for the assurance that liberates us from fear, doubt, the turmoil of the world, the apprehension of danger, and from the vagaries of men. Only when we have cast off the self-limiting conditions and self-defeating behaviors that blind us to a larger view of life, will we enjoy a settled conviction of the truth in our minds. The peace that follows obedience to celestial principles brings a greater reality within our reach. When we realize that we are not alone, we have begun a journey that will carry us to a higher state of being where we will find ourselves covered in star dust, as we mingle with the Gods.

> We are baptized that we might pause,
> and reflect upon the things that
> are really important
> in our lives.

Whose reflection do we see when we look down into the still waters of baptism?

Reflection is a good thing, especially when it is Christ Who is the tangible source of the light. As Alma asked the people of Zarahemla, "And now, behold, I ask of you, my brethren of the church, have ye spiritually been born of God? Have ye received His image in your countenances? Have ye experienced this mighty change in your heart?" (Alma 5:14).

What kind of change comes over us at our baptism?

With the image of the Lord in our countenance, our faces reflect the light of Christ. When we experience a mighty change in our hearts, we will be transformed, not by maturation, but by generation, to become new creatures in Christ.

How does the world seek change?

The world attempts to make changes from the outside, and fails miserably. The Gospel changes us from the inside, and succeeds brilliantly. We are thus created to reach our potential in both the image and likeness of God, our Father.

Why is the worship of idols of any kind so destructive?

Idol worship is the epitome of taking the name of God in vain. One of the terrible consequences of the fascination of Babylon with idols is spiritual insensitivity. Isaiah foresaw the Last Days, when he wrote: "Stay yourselves, and wonder; cry ye out, and cry: they are drunken, but not with wine; they stagger, but not with strong drink. For the Lord hath poured out upon you the spirit of deep sleep, and hath closed your eyes: the prophets, and your rulers, and seers hath he covered." (Isaiah 29:9-21).

46.

> We are baptized that we
> might affirm our faith in the
> immortality of our souls, because
> we feel, within ourselves,
> immortal longings.

What does it mean that we are spiritual beings having mortal experiences?

With Enos, we "rejoice in the day when (our) mortal shall put on immortality, and shall stand before him; then shall (we) see his face with pleasure, and he will say unto (us): Come unto me, ye blessed, there is a place prepared for you in the mansions of my Father." (Enos 1:27).

What does it feel like when the veil seems to be very thin?

Sometimes, when we brush against the veil, we feel inner stirrings that are the harmonic vibrations of music from a heavenly choir, and we hear the indistinct voices of angelic messengers. This is one of the reasons that we are baptized; that even as we dwell on the earth, we might be blessed to be "partakers of the divine nature." (2 Peter 1:4).

What is magical about putting our lives in harmony with the principles of The Plan?

There are rhythms in nature that can be felt only when we are in harmony with eternal principles. The veil can be almost transparent when we are spiritually sensitive. As our powers expand, we enjoy the glittering facets of the life of the Spirit, until we feel that we have been cast off into a stream of revelation and carried along in the quickening currents of direct experience with God.

Why was the commandment to be baptized given, in the first place?

"For this end was the law given," to prepare us to be more like the Savior, until "we are made alive in (Him) because of our faith." (2 Nephi 25:25, see Matthew 5:48).

47.

We are baptized that we might learn to abide by the laws of the Celestial Kingdom, even as we dwell upon the earth, that our hearts might burn within us, as the Spirit speaks to us and opens the scriptures to our understanding.
(See Luke 24:32).

What can happen to us if we wait another day to take advantage of repentance?

We must not put off developing saving faith until we have become spiritually dead to the Light of Christ. To do so, exposes us to the wiles of the devil, because we are no longer able to make the vital distinctions between good and evil, or between light and darkness. (See Alma 34:35).

What happens if we neglect to rely upon the Atonement through repentance?

The Spirit of the Lord withdraws and the devil has power over the children of men, when they voluntarily surrender to him their freedom to act independently. This is the state of the unrepentant wicked, from which there may be no recovery. When the sword of justice falls, it will be for them as if there had been no redemption made, and the Atonement will be of no effect. (See Alma 34:35).

What happens when the wicked have no intention of repenting?

When depravity drives away the Spirit, and the lives of the wicked are thrown into imbalance, chaos and ruin are the inevitable result. The tragedy is not what becomes of them, but what they themselves have become.

Do you think angels notice our obedience to the laws of heaven?

As the battle rages in the hearts of men, those who have been baptized will live their lives in crescendo. The deafening roar of their righteousness will command the attention of the angels who wield the sword of justice and who await God's command to let it fall on an unrepentant world.

We are baptized that we might think less in terms of self-sufficiency, and more about our Christ dependency.

What do you think it means to "come unto Christ?" (Moroni 10:32).

We realize that His message was intended to change not only our behavior, but also our nature. Perfect obedience to the laws and ordinances of the Gospel qualifies us to enter into the Rest of the Lord. Our covenants have the power to move us along the path of progression to the point that we reflect God's divine attributes. These are some of the reasons why we take the Sacrament weekly, and repetitively rehearse the veil experience as part of the temple endowment.

How can we emulate divine attributes after our baptism?

We can be chaste in our behavior and love others. We can discipline our nature, and be righteous stewards. We can love our less fortunate brethren. We can take proper care of our bodies, and try to stay in touch with the Spirit. We can pray to understand the gift of His Son, and we can ponder the power of His priesthood by participating in the ordinances of the Gospel.

How does baptism prepare us deal with the challenges of life?

By living in accordance with the principles of the Gospel, we begin to understand how our covenants with God help us to overcome adversity and gain self-mastery. As we do so, it begins to dawn on us that this is the purpose of the covenants we make with Him. With a quickening pulse, we begin to understand that our covenants prepare us to become as He is.

How is the Savior the sole source of our protection?

He has promised us: "There is no weapon that is formed against you shall prosper." (D&C 71:9). If we keep our covenants, He will cause the heavens to shake for our good, "and Satan shall tremble and Zion shall rejoice upon the hills and flourish." (D&C 35:24).

49.

> We are baptized that we might be given the tools to burst free of our self-imposed limitations.

What happens to us when we keep the Savior in our thoughts?

When the Savior is the focus of our lives, the clarity of our vision gives us the ability to overcome our weaknesses. Stumbling blocks become stepping stones, and experience teaches us that "all things which are good cometh of Christ." (Moroni 7:24).

What happens to us when we lose the guidance of the Holy Ghost?

If we mistakenly trivialize celestial sureties, we become susceptible to temporal trivialities and the suffocating storms of telestial tempests. If we lower our defensive shield of faith, we become vulnerable to the lethal storms sweeping the face of the earth, that have been generated by the destroyer of worlds to suck life-sustaining marrow from the bones of the unwary.

What happens to us when we are attuned to the whisperings of the Spirit?

The powers of heaven and earth amplify each other, and carry us along on waves of the Spirit. With baptism, all our trappings and pretenses are shorn away, and outward observances and phylacteries are stripped from the ritual of our worship, leaving only our true feelings.

Why do we use the expression: "The healing waters of baptism?"

Raw and ugly sores that have been inflicted by worldly influences are healed in the waters of baptism. The Balm of Gilead prevails over even the most traumatic soul scars that are the result of our confrontations with Babylon.

50.

We are baptized in consequence of the "evils and designs which do and will exist in the hearts of conspiring men (and women) in the last days." (D&C 89:4).

How does baptism invite the protection of heaven?

Angels will attend us after we have entered the Fold. "For I will go before your face," promised the Lord. "I will be on your right hand, and on your left, and my Spirit shall be in your hearts, and mine angels round about you, to bear you up." (D&C 84:88).

How does baptism pad our spiritual bank accounts?

We are all faced with times when withdrawals must be made from our spiritual bank accounts. Because of our covenant consciousness, however, we do not write checks that cannot be cashed. We faithfully and consistently make deposits over a period of time, so that we can count upon the cornucopia of comfort created by the cushion of confidence that courses from consistently conforming our conduct to covenants contracted with our Creator.

How can we be protected against the comprehensive and organized forces of evil?

Simply put, baptism introduces us to the process by which we may progress. Heavenly Father designed baptism to test our mettle. This is why having the courage to be true to our convictions is so intimately tied to righteousness. Only when we act on the basis of faith will we receive a confirmation of the power behind the ordinance of baptism, as feelings of self-confidence grow and purposeful action replaces our tentative overtures.

What is our best defense against evil?

The relevancy of King Benjamin's counsel is almost self-evident: "This much I can tell you," he said. "If ye do not watch yourselves, and your thoughts, and your words, and your deeds, and observe the commandments of God, and continue in the faith...even unto the end of your lives, ye must perish." (Mosiah 4:30).

51.

We are baptized that we might publish peace and tidings
of great joy, endure to the end, and be lifted up at
the last day, to inherit eternal life.
(See 1 Nephi 13:37).

How does the Gospel bring the world news of great joy and peace?

Aaron taught King Lamoni's father: "Since man had fallen, he could not merit anything of himself; but the sufferings and death of Christ atone for their sins, through faith and repentance, (and) he breaketh the bands of death, that the grave shall have no victory...that the sting of death should be swallowed up in the hopes of glory" (Alma 22:14).

What happens to us as we publish peace and glad tidings?

Because we are at risk of the constant and unrelenting assaults of Satan upon our spiritual identities, we must cling to the belief that only our Heavenly Father can maintain our spiritual health. We must be ready to turn over our lives to His care and keeping, as we publish peace. We must constantly monitor the stability and integrity of our moral shields, as we bear glad tidings. When we meet Satan on the field of battle, we must be ready to acknowledge our reliance upon the matchless power of God.

How can we generate the spiritual horsepower to worship the Savior with fervency?

Think of the occasion when Jesus asked the Pharisees: "What think ye of Christ? Whose son is he?" (Matthew 22:41-42). Sadly, their sluggish response was tendered with little feeling or emotion. Its dearth of traction was obvious, its inability to generate spontaneity was palpable, its lack of energy to engage enthusiasm was noticeable, its incapacity to kindle vitality was evident, and its failure to candidly acknowledge the powerful relationship that can exist between ourselves and God was clear.

How can we strengthen our relationship with the Savior?

The simple questions: "What think ye of Christ?" demands that we dig deeply within ourselves before we bear our witness, because it is all too easy to superficially retreat into colorless and insipid verbiage as the easy way out. If we casually and carelessly steer a course away from Him with offhand, dismissive, and inconsiderate comments, until He is conveniently out of sight, mind, and spirit, we can realistically expect in return no more than a stupor of thought.

52.

> We are baptized that we might
> enjoy the Sabbath day, as
> we never have before.

How does baptism help us to obey the Law of the Sabbath?

Baptism exposes us to a variety of spiritual gifts that can be the antidote for the poisonous telestial tendencies that suppress the comprehension of celestial sureties. God has given us a day of worship and of rest, that we may repose far from the madding crowd. He knows that it is easy for us to choke on possessions whose opacity clouds our ability to experience illumination by the Spirit. Focusing on the kingdom, especially on the Sabbath day, helps us to maintain our perspective, which strengthens our reverence for His work.

For what purpose was the Sabbath day created?

God has prepared the Sabbath day as a "work release program" to see how we will behave when we are left on our own, after having received unambiguous instruction regarding what we ought to do with His day of rest from our labors.

How can baptism help the Sabbath day become more special?

On His day, we "praise (His) great and terrible name, for it is holy." (Psalms 99:3). Those who profane or secularize the Sabbath are no longer put to death, and yet we die spiritually when we alienate ourselves from God's influence, because our progression comes to a halt. For "broad is the gate, and wide they way that leadeth to the deaths; and many there are that go in thereat, because they receive me not, neither do they abide in my law." (D&C 132:25).

How can baptism turn our hearts to the Law of The Sabbath?

There is a perpetual battle raging in our hearts. It pits our desire to serve our Master against telestial tendencies that twist our focus inward, toward ourselves and away from our Creator. "Two ways always lie open before us - one leading to an ever lower and lower plane, where are heard the cries of despair and the curses of the poor, where manhood shrivels and possessions wear down the possessor; and the other leading to the highlands of the morning where are heard the glad shouts of humanity, and where honest effort is rewarded with immortality." (John P. Altgeld).

53.

We are baptized that we might reconnect with our spiritual Birth Parents.

Day-by-day, how can we maintain a connection with the eternities?

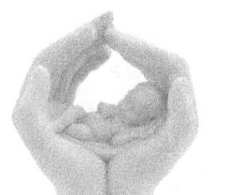

When we came from the eternal vantage point of the abode of the Gods, the celestial clock, insofar as we are concerned, was reset. Time was inserted into The Plan, in order to allow us to enjoy a temporal matrix within which we could work out our salvation before the Lord. At least for now, the arrow of time moves relentlessly forward, moving us ever closer to our date with destiny. Its passage provides context within which The Plan may unfold its mysteries to those who have been prepared, through baptism, to catch a glimpse of eternity.

How does our baptism expand our understanding of our divine heritage?

We see the scriptures in a new light, that we "are the sons" and daughters "of the living God." (Hosea 1:10). "The Spirit itself beareth witness with our spirit, that we are the children of God." (Romans 8:16). We find answers to our yearning to know: "Have we not all one father?" In the face of overwhelming evidence, we ask the rhetorical question: "Hath not one God created us?" (Malachi 2:10).

How does God answer, when we ask: "Father, are you there?"

In a wonderfully whole and complete manner, Heavenly Father is sensitive to our needs and to our prayers, however small or insignificant they may seem to us. He does hear us, because prayer draws upon His virtue. Every time we reach out to Him, we are, in effect, touching the Savior's garment. How we do this, no one can describe, for it must be directly experienced. (See Mark 5:27-34).

How is our baptism related to the sealing power of the priesthood?

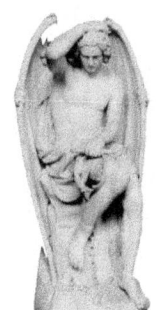

If we remain true to our covenants, there will be no empty chairs around the table at family reunions in the eternities. When we return home from our mortal mission, we will fondly remember the people we met, and those we helped. We will recall how we have grown both physically and spiritually. We will find Mother there, waiting to embrace us, as She stands beside Father, Who will be bursting with pride. She will brush away the tears of happiness on our cheeks. Father will strike hands with us, and then hug us tenderly. Mother will put Her arm around our waist, and escort us to the familiar surroundings that have been prepared for our homecoming.

We are baptized that we might enter into God's Rest.

How is God's Rest harmonious with family exaltation?

Our families can be our greatest source of joy in time, as well as in the eternities. In moments of deep reflection, as at the waters of baptism, we envision "stepping on shore, and finding it heaven! We visualize taking hold of a hand, and finding it God's hand. We contemplate breathing a new air, and finding it celestial air. We imagine feeling invigorated, and finding it immortality. We dream of passing from storm and tempest to an unbroken calm, and of waking up, and finding it home." (Anonymous).

How can baptism generate the power to propel us into God's Rest?

Moroni promised: "If it so be that ye believe in Christ, and are baptized, first with water, then with fire and with the Holy Ghost, following the example of our Savior, according to that which he hath commanded us, it shall be well with you in the day of judgment." (Mormon 7:10).

What must we do, in order to be able to enter into God's Rest?

When we gain a perfect knowledge of the divinity of the work, we will no longer suffer from fear, doubt, apprehension of danger, the religious turmoil of the world, or from the vagaries of men. His Rest is born of a settled conviction of the truth in our minds, and is manifest in the peace that follows our obedience to celestial principles.

After our baptism, how can we reach out and touch the face of God?

As we make our way through "this vale of tears," the real journey to Christ has only just begun. (See Wycliffe's Bible, Psalms 84:6). Having been born again through baptism, we must continue to press forward with complete dedication and steadfastness, with confidence and with a firm determination in Christ, having a perfect brightness of hope, or perfect faith, and charity, or a love of God and of our brothers and sisters.

55.

We are baptized that we might
vitalize Heavenly Father's
Plan of Happiness
in our lives.

What can we do to internalize the principles that lead to happiness?

Joseph Smith said: "Happiness is the object and design of our existence, and will be the end thereof, if we pursue the path that leads to it, and this path is virtue, uprightness, faithfulness, holiness, and keeping all of the commandments of God."

How does our baptism provide opportunities to re-adjust our priorities?

With baptism, some of us painfully recognize that we have sought "all the days of (our) lives for that which (we) cannot obtain, and...have sought for happiness in doing iniquity, which thing is contrary to the nature of that righteousness which is in our great and Eternal Head." (Helaman 13:38). Enlightened by the Spirit, the eyes of our understanding are opened, and we can see more clearly the path that lies before us. (See D&C 76:12, 110:1, and 138:11).

Why is the Gospel the foundation of real happiness?

Baptism provides insight into the spiritual roots of our relationships, and into happiness, that is the product of interconnectivity and interdependence. This helps us to live in the world without being tarnished by it. In the end, "abundance is multiplied unto (the Saints) through the manifestations of the Spirit." (D&C 70:13). Our righteous objectives stay in focus when we pay attention to the guideposts that have been provided by our Heavenly Father. These mile markers help us to deflect the grit and grime that can accumulate during our journey through mortality.

Why do those who disobey the commandments sometimes seem to be happy?

Many live "after the manner of happiness for a season." They are able to do this because their level of understanding and their behavior harmonize with worldly values. As long as they can shut out the light of Christ, they may live the illusion. But, sooner or later, the discrepancy between their behavior and Gospel ideals will become so great that it cannot be sustained, and their short-lived pleasure in worldly ways will be destroyed. They will ultimately realize that "wickedness never was happiness." (Alma 41:10).

> We are baptized that we might forever
> thereafter commemorate
> the birthdate of our
> immortal souls.

Why is our baptism a cause for celebration in heaven?

Bathed in the stunning clarity of light, those who have been baptized often stare in wide-eyed wonder at the beautiful simplicity of the interwoven threads within the pattern of Gospel principles that make up the tapestry of The Plan of Salvation. This is in sharp contrast to the slit-eyed skepticism with which the unrepentant and hard-hearted greet the truth.

How does the day of our baptism commemorate the birthdate of our immortal soul?

With baptism, we choose liberty and eternal life, instead of captivity and spiritual death. We choose to live our lives within the context of the Gospel and its laws; without it, our unbridled freedom would lead to tyranny. We are free to choose whether or not we wish to be baptized, but we cannot choose to escape the consequences of poor decision-making. It is Christ's way for us to act for ourselves. (See 2 Nephi 2:27). It is Satan's way for us to be acted upon. Because of the Atonement, the 'perfect law of liberty' allows us to be free according to the flesh. (See James 1:25).

What kind of a message does baptism send to heaven?

Baptism opens a portal to the principles, ordinances, and covenants that enable us to become sanctified, so that we may be worthy to live once again in a state of holiness in the presence of our Heavenly Father. Because of baptism, all may come unto Christ, and lay hold upon every good gift...and be perfected in him, (as they) deny (themselves) of all ungodliness." (Moroni 10:30 & 32). Because of baptism, we may all "continue in the supplicating of his grace" to one day stand blameless before Him at His Pleasing Bar. (See Alma 7:3).

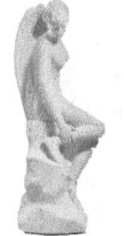

Do you think that heavenly beings are given permission to attend baptismal services?

When we stand in holy places and free ourselves from the cares and concerns of the world, the realities of the eternities illuminate our minds. At our baptism, if we listen very carefully, we can hear the gentle rustling of the wings of angels coming from behind a slightly-parted veil. The company of beings from the unseen world sweeps the cobwebs from our minds and opens up to our view undreamed vistas of otherwise inaccessible experience.

We are baptized that we might have hope in our Savior, Jesus Christ.

How does our knowledge of The Plan expand the scope of our hope in Christ?

Baptism compels us to consider the possibility that we might one day be like the Savior. We believe that His grace consists of the gifts and power by which we may be brought to His perfection and stature, so that we may enjoy not only what He has, but also what He is. We believe in His promise: "If ye by the grace of God are perfect in Christ, and deny not his power, then are ye sanctified in Christ by the grace of God, through the shedding of the blood of Christ, which is in the covenant of the Father unto the remission of your sins, that ye become holy, without spot." (Moroni 10:33).

Is hope in Christ reserved only for members of His Church?

Baptism is not prejudicial; it simply levels the playing field for all of Heavenly Father's children. He has enough confidence in The Plan to allows our agency to find expression in myriad ways. The ordinances that are part of The Plan will always stand ready to save our souls, but in the meantime, we may worship Almighty God according to the dictates of our conscience. The "Author of Eternal Salvation" allows us to worship how, where, or what we may. (Hebrews 5:9, see the 11th Article of Faith).

How can baptism make Saints of sinners?

The distinctions between members and non-members, active and inactive individuals, adult Aaronic and Melchizedek priesthood bearers, or single, divorced, widowed, and married people matter very little. Saints and sinners are not so very different, after all. Baptism is the great equalizer. (See Acts 10:34).

How does baptism reflect our hope in Christ?

Hope is not misguided trust in promises that cannot be fulfilled, nor is it a high stakes gamble based on statistical improbabilities. It is the inevitable reward of well-founded faith, when we have developed the discipline to completely control desires and emotions within the bounds the Lord has set, and when our priorities are in harmony with Gospel principles.

> We are baptized in a process of generation,
> and not just of maturation.
> (See Mosiah 27:26).

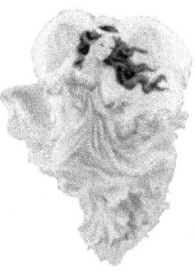

How is baptism a mile post on our journey to Christ?

Mortality has been designed to be a life-long learning laboratory to give each of us the opportunity to mold our nature to more closely resemble that of our Father in Heaven. He initiated baptism to make that metamorphosis possible.

What does it mean to make the journey to Christ?

Baptism is the catalyst that propels us upward toward discovery of the personal levels of experience with the Savior, for when He speaks of "knowing Him," He must be referring to a special sense of the word. It is not enough that we know about Him by reading the Gospels, or by listening to others speak of Him. We must know Him through the bonds of common experience and common feeling.

How does baptism bind us to Heavenly Father's perfect Plan of Salvation?

Our religion is more involved with recovery than discovery. Our destiny is not union, but reunion with divine realities. Our religious recognition is a re-learning of that which we have already understood. In this context, the word religion may derive from the Latin root "ligare" – "to bind." Thus, religion would mean "to bind again." This harmonizes with the perspective linking religion to a reunion with a divine purpose, or a Plan, for Heavenly Father's children.

How does baptism illustrate the genius of our Heavenly Fathers' Plan?

Baptism represents more than the making of resolutions that can be nothing more than promises to ourselves that are generally kept for a few days or weeks at best, before they are abandoned and we return to our previously held lifestyles. The ordinance of baptism has staying power. Baptism has no bias; its basis is belief, nurtured by the rich culture medium of faith, repentance and the companionship of the Spirit. (See the 4th Article of Faith).

59.

> We are baptized that we might enter into
> the fold, there to be cared for
> by the Good Shepherd.
> (See John 10:11).

Why can we not allow ourselves to be complacent about our baptismal covenant?

"We have paused on some plateaus long enough," declared President Spencer W. Kimball. "Let us resume our journey forward and upward. Let us quietly put an end to our reluctance to reach out to others, whether in our own families, wards, or neighborhoods. We have been diverted at times from fundamentals on which we must now focus, in order to move forward as a person or as a people." (C.R., April 1979).

How is baptism the gift that keeps on giving?

For many, following their baptism, the feelings they would like to express cannot be formed into words. Suffice to say, that by the grace of their Heavenly Father, their eyes have been opened. The Savior becomes their traveling companion and confidant. He helps them to forget their bad days and to become better; to love their families, and to be more responsible towards others. In a word, to sacrifice themselves through the love of the Lord.

How does baptism re-define itself each time the faithful enter the healing water?

With our baptism, gone are the days when we would have been content to build upon the sepulchres of the fathers. For too long, the world has been satisfied writing only biographies, histories, and criticisms relating to the mission of the Savior. But we are no longer comfortable with only these third-person accounts. The restored authority to baptize stands as a testament that, once again, it is possible to individually, and not only institutionally, tap directly into the fountain of living water.

How does baptism help us to live in accordance with priesthood principles?

As soon as we learn to govern our lives by the eternally valid principles of The Plan of Salvation, we will find ourselves on the path that leads to God's kingdom. John Taylor correctly taught: "Priesthood is the legitimate rule of God and is the only power that has a right to rule upon the earth, and when His will is done on the earth, as it is done in heaven, no other power will bear rule." (J.D. 5:187).

We are baptized that we might contribute our own chapter to The Greatest Story Ever Told.

What will be the reaction of those who sit down to read your chapter in The Greatest Story Ever Told?

The Greatest Story Ever Told was meant to be a sign and a wonder to an unbelieving world. It was designed to give guidance to true believers in the Last Days. It is a story for hard times and for good times. It has the power to dismiss worldly influences that compete with its issues of real substance that should be the focus of our attention.

What tools have we been given to help us to richly illustrate our own chapters in The Greatest Story Ever Told?

David O. McKay taught that the time between our birth and the age of accountability is ideally suited to learning the principles of the Gospel. In fact, children are like little sponges, effortlessly soaking up the doctrines of the kingdom.

How have your mentors modified their approach, when teaching you how to write your story?

President McKay taught that the time between their ninth and seventeenth year is the ideal period for children to be trained in the application of the principles of the Gospel that had been previously taught at home and in Church.

How does The Plan of Salvation set us free to reach our potential?

President McKay taught that when they reach the age of sixteen, it is time for those who will soon be young adults to be trusted in the correct application of the principles they have been taught, that have formed the basis of their training, and that have been incorporated, through practice, into their lives.

61.

> We are baptized that our Heavenly
> Father might create, in our behalf,
> an impenetrable "shield of faith"
> in our Lord Jesus Christ.
> (Ephesians 6:16).

Why do you think we are baptized individually, and not in large groups?

A heavenly armourer has fitted each of us with a shield of faith. It has been tailored to our unique and distinctive needs. Its elements are composed of the covenants we make with Heavenly Father. We make these individually, and not collectively, and we renew them repetitively. This protects us from getting caught up in the mechanics of the Church, from killing the articles of its faith, or from permitting form to triumph over spirit. The kingdom can then be built by something as simple as our ardor and conviction, as we consciously nurture our relationship with heaven in a process that formally begins with our baptism.

Why is it important to keep our shields of faith bright and shiny?

By its very nature, baptism contributes to "a great division among the people." (2 Nephi 30:10). In these Last Days, our adversaries are jockeying for position to control our minds, just as they did during our pre-mortal existence. Once again, combatants with increasingly polarized ideologies are forming ranks as they go to battle. (See Revelation 16:14).

How do our shields of faith encourage accountability?

Baptism banishes ignorance, for all will one day stand accountable for their own decisions. "There is no eye that shall not see, neither ear that shall not hear, neither heart that shall not be penetrated." (DC 1:2). "The voice of warning (shall) be unto all people," and "those who reject the glad message, the rebellious, shall be pierced with much sorrow." (D&C 1:3-4).

Why is baptism integral to our shields of faith?

Baptism is the supernal example of the exercise of our agency, but it almost compels us to internalize Gospel principles. It teaches us to view our lives from an eternal perspective, which makes it easier to discern the polarized opposites that are so prevalent in our society today. When we see through the clarifying lens of faith, we can more easily distinguish happiness from its worldly counterfeits, such as pleasure, desire, indulgence, decadence, sensuality, gratification, carnality, amusement, and simply having "fun." Baptism makes it possible to live in the world and to be weighed in the balances without being found wanting. (See Daniel 5:27).

> We are baptized in white clothing,
> to symbolically express the
> purity of the ordinance
> and the proximity
> of the Spirit.

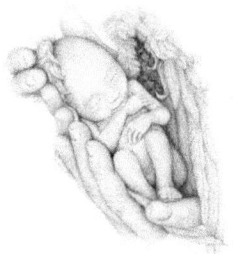

Why do we wear white clothing at baptismal services?

It comes down to the guidance and instruction we receive in the "General Handbook of Instructions 2 (20.3.6): "A person who performs a baptism and a person who is baptized wear white clothing."

Are those who administer the Sacrament required to wear white clothing?

No, they are not. However, as Jeffrey R. Holland taught: "For sacred ordinances in the Church, we often use ceremonial clothing, and a white shirt could be seen as a gentle reminder of the white clothing you wore in the baptismal font and in anticipation of the white shirt you will soon wear into the temple and onto your missions." (C.R., 10/1995).

Is there an official Church policy or standard that requires the wearing of white clothing at times other than when performing the baptismal ordinance?

White may be the preferable color of shirt worn by those who administer the sacrament, (but not by those who receive it). However, with the exception of temple clothing, which is generally white, (think of those who witness live sealing ordinances, who simply wear their "Sunday best"), members of the Church may decide for themselves, through the direction of the Spirit, what they believe is appropriate to wear.

How can baptism help us to have clean hands and pure hearts? (See Psalms 24:4).

Though the wearing of white is encouraged while administering the sacrament, it is not required. President David O. McKay expressed the desire that those who do not have a white shirt might come to the Sacrament table "with clean hands, and especially with a pure heart...anything that will make the young boys feel that they have been called to officiate in the Priesthood in one of the most sacred ordinances in the Church" (C.R., 10/1956).

63.

> We are baptized that the Spirit of the Lord Omnipotent might work "a mighty change in us, or in our hearts, that we have no more disposition to do evil, but to do good continually."
> (Mosiah 5:2).

How does knowing that we are God's children change our behavior?

Our religious recognition is a re-cognition, a re-knowing, the sum of our existence. Baptism helps us to nurture that intuitive response. If we thwart our intrinsic light, "we are accountable, and to a degree, we condemn ourselves. We knew Christ before this life, we know Him here, and we will know Him hereafter. His sheep do indeed know His voice." (Truman Madsen).

How do we view the world when our nature has been changed through baptism?

Those who demand outward evidence of the power of God as a condition for their belief seek to circumvent the process by which both faith and knowledge are developed. They want proof without price. As with the adulterer, they seek the result without accepting the responsibility, or the steak without the sizzle.

Why does faith always precede the miracle?

Baptism was not conceived to follow the receipt of signs from heaven. Instead, our faith precedes the miracle. We must take a few steps into the darkness, and then the spiritual strong searchlight will illuminate the way. Spiritual confirmation always flows along the course that has been created by faith. If a witness were given before faith had transformed us, we might have sure knowledge. But it would have come without an expenditure of faith, and so there would be no appreciation of its significance. It is faith that infuses our belief with staying power.

How does our baptism kindle vital faith?

Baptism grounds us to practical belief, but with elements that commit us to an upward thrust. However, our subsequent works do not assure us of salvation, nor do they make us good; it is our faith that does so. Wresting the scriptures, by suggesting that we are saved by works, twists holy writ from its true or proper signification, and perverts it from its correct application. Our faith notwithstanding, we are saved by the grace of God, after all we can do. (See 2 Nephi 25:23).

> We are baptized "through the infinite goodness of God,
> (that by) the manifestations of his Spirit (we might)
> have great views of that which is to come."
> (Mosiah 5:3).

How is our spiritual education different from worldly learning?

Rather than simply multiplying mirrors and studying angles without increasing the light, the first principles and ordinances of the Gospel facilitate the illumination of our minds by the Spirit.

What happens when we allow the Spirit to teach us?

We have no proof until we act on the basis of belief. Then comes the ratification of the reality manifest as spiritual confirmation, but only after we act in faith. That is the essence of why James taught that "faith, if it hath not works, is dead, being alone." (James 2:17).

How does baptism have the power to change behavior?

Baptism is the evidence of our exercise of faith. We mature spiritually until our faith becomes perfect knowledge. Initially, faith is to believe what we do not see, and the reward of faith is to see what we believe. The process by which faith is developed is one of testing. The Lord gives certain principles, and by obedience to them, blessings and power follow.

What happens to those who wait upon the Lord? (See Isaiah 40:31).

The marvel of God's love is that the more we try to serve Him, the more He blesses us. Therefore, we become even more deeply indebted to Him, and remain so forever. That debt is completely beyond our ability to pay. We can do nothing that puts Him in our debt. But God does not ask us to settle our account with Him; He only asks that we obey Him, beginning with His commandment to be baptized.

65.

> We are baptized that we might evenly distribute
> the weight of our temporal baggage, that
> we might more easily "enter in
> at the strait gate."
> (Matthew 7:13).

How can we more comfortably carry our burdens?

Temporal baggage can create imbalance that leads to confusion. Baptism jars us out of our collective complacency by upsetting the stagnation of the status quo. It invites us to enjoy a settled conviction in our minds of the truth, by getting our juices flowing, prodding us to constructively expend our energy, and judiciously putting our agency to work.

How can temporal baggage get in the way of our spiritual objectives?

Brigham Young taught: "The first principle that ought to occupy our attention and which is the mainspring of all action is the principle of improvement," and this requires us to balance our temporal baggage with our spiritual objectives and not to confuse one for the other.

How do you think the Lord views our temporal baggage?

Our grasp of the riches of eternity may be something as simple as our ability to see from the perspective of our Heavenly Father. Our covenants, beginning with baptism, expand our vision beyond physical laws that pertain only to the temporal world, toward an appreciation of Gospel principles that relate to the eternities. Baptism invites us to reach out and touch the face of God, not with our fingers, but with our faith.

How can baptism help us to avoid being tainted by temporal baggage?

We may live in the world as long as our feet are firmly planted on Gospel sod and we recognize sounding brass and tinkling cymbals for what they really are. Baptism catalyzes a mystical and metaphysical transformation wherein we are figuratively born of God, so that we can see more clearly with new eyes. (See Mosiah 5:7).

> We are baptized that the
> "opposition in all things" to which Lehi
> alluded, might become a blessing that
> allows us to more fully engage
> The Plan of Salvation.
> (2 Nephi 2:11).

How can our baptism become the foundation for purposeful action?

At our baptism, we are given an extra measure of resolve to see life through to its successful conclusion. When that course seems confusing because it has been complicated by opposition, Gospel principles stand ready to counter the conundrum.

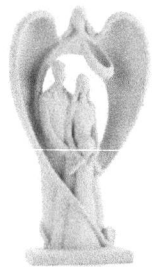

How can baptism help us to view opposition as a blessing in disguise?

A lot depends upon how we handle opposition, and on what we allow it to do to us. It may impede our progress; but on the other hand, we may use it as a stepping-stone to higher achievement. Our baptism can give us the perspective to see adversity as a diamond dust that polishes us to a high luster, rather than as an abrasive that wears us down and grinds us up.

How can we engage the elements of The Plan when dealing with opposition?

President Heber J. Grant once said: "If we are trying, to the best of our ability, to improve day by day, then we are in the line of our duty. If we are seeking to remedy our own defects, if we are so living that we can ask for light, for knowledge, for intelligence, and above all, for His Spirit that we may overcome weakness, then, I can tell you, we are in the straight and narrow path that leads to life eternal."

How does the Savior help us to manage opposition?

Opposition can weaken us if we do not hearken to the counsel of the Savior. We are quickened by baptism, that we might use opposition as the key it was intended to be, to throw open a portal to the Spirit. We thereby internalize Gospel principles, and in our obedience to priesthood covenants, we may accomplish all things. (See Philippians 4:13).

67.

We are baptized
that our trials and tribulations
might give us experience, and
work to our benefit.
(See D&C 122:7).

How does baptism help us to reach our potential in the learning laboratory of life?

"Baptism of repentance for the remission of sins," (Luke 3:3), together with the Sacrament, fuels our actions, charges our spiritual batteries, and energizes our vision with infinite perspective, creating a pulsing stream of inspiration, whose flow has no temporal or spatial boundary. We are swept up by quickening currents into the direct experience of a holy communion with God.

How can our baptism help us to see more clearly from an eternal perspective?

When designing the Plan, God knew that, with only nine months of preparation, we would transition from the eternal world where we had enjoyed the warmth of hearth and home in heaven, to the bleak atmosphere of the lone and dreary world here on earth, and that when we did so, there would be an immediate disconnect that would be brutal and unrelenting in its intensity. In order to cope with that unforgiving reality check, God made it instinctively possible for us to enjoy connections with eternity that would gently lead us toward the waters of baptism.

How can our baptism help us to increase our spiritually aerobic maximum pulse rate, as well as the capacity of our lungs to fill with celestial air?

Those who submit to baptism almost immediately experience an earth shaking and mind bending theophany. They are jolted, not by the shock of the water against their skin, but instead by the sober realization that they are the spiritual offspring of deity. As they come up out of the font, they begin to recognize the potential of their position.

How can baptism help us to be comfortable in the company of immortal beings?

A kinetic energy defines our relationship with Christ. It is generated by our dynamic worship that is fueled by the fire of faith. We who are about to be baptized manifest ourselves as white hot sparks struck of the divine anvil of God. Quenched in the waters of healing, we emerge as tempered steel, in a mystical transformation that can only be described as being "born again."

68.

> We are baptized that the "redemption exemption," that is a codicil to the Law of Justice, might be activated and the Law of Mercy set in motion, as our lease on life is renegotiated in our favor.

Why do you think Heavenly Father and the Holy Ghost are present at baptisms?

All who enter the waters of baptism do so by divine design, because they are the nobility of heaven. They are counted among those of a choice and chosen generation. (See 1 Peter 2:9). The baptism of Jesus was attended by the greatest Witnesses of all, Heavenly Father and the Holy Ghost, and so, when the ordinance is performed in our day, the names of all three members of the Godhead are similarly invoked, to witness their validation of our very special Lease on Life.

Following baptism, how can we take advantage of our own brand new lease on life?

We are baptized because none of us would choose to become spiritually depleted, or to perish because of our neglect of the things that matter most. We understand the consequences of spiritual starvation, doctrinal dehydration, and intellectual inhibition. Without baptism, we risk living marginalized lives while only inches away from the living bread that would have satisfied our hunger, and from the healing fountain of truth that could have slaked our thirst.

How can we enhance to our benefit the terms of our Lease on Life?

As we think about our baptism, perhaps we will intuitively respond to President Gordon B. Hinckley's invitation to do a little better, to be a little more kind, to be a little more merciful, and a little more forgiving; "to put behind us our weaknesses of the past, and go forth with new energy and increased resolution to improve the world about us, in our homes, in our places of employment," and "in our social activities."

How does baptism strengthen our resolve to be true to our divine destiny?

The covenant is a token of our understanding and acceptance of the principles of The Plan of Salvation, and of our determination to remain faithful to our Father in Heaven. We think of brave Horatius, the captain of the gate, who declared: "To every man upon this earth, death cometh soon or late. And how can man die better than facing fearful odds, for the ashes of his fathers, and the temples of his gods?" (Thomas Babbington McCaulay).

69.

> We are baptized that
> we might make a simple public
> statement about a profound
> private conviction.

In what ways can our baptism be unassuming and reflective?

If we learn to love, we'll love to live, and our charity will become infectious.

How does our faith transport us beyond the words of the ordinance to a spiritual covenant with God?

Our baptism focuses our attention on our testimonies, and the covenant encourages us to nurture them. Every day thereafter, we take our testimony temperature, and hope to regularly detect its feverish pitch. As Alma asked: "Have ye spiritually been born of God? Have ye received his image in your countenances? Have ye experienced this mighty change in your hearts?" (Alma 6:14).

Do the baptismal prayer and sacrament prayers need to be delivered with exactness?

The General Handbook of Instructions 2.20.1 states: "When ordinances or blessings are performed in sacrament meeting, the bishop ensures that they are performed properly. To avoid embarrassing a priesthood holder, the bishop quietly corrects errors only if <u>essential elements</u> of the ordinance or blessing are incorrect." (Underlining mine). In the baptismal prayer, however, it is necessary to recite the words with precision.

How is it possible that the 25 simple words of the baptismal prayer can have such profound meaning?

As we respond to the invitation to enter into the fold, the Spirit moves upon us to wash our flesh in water, anoint our bodies with oil, and put on holy garments, that we might be prepared to enter the joy of the Lord. (See Leviticus 16:4, Exodus 40:12-13 & Matthew 25:21).

> We are baptized "that we might speak with the tongue of angels, and shout praises unto the Holy One of Israel." (2 Nephi 31:13).

How do you think baptism prepares us to receive spiritual gifts?

We cannot purchase spiritual gifts with the treasures of the earth. Perhaps this is why in their efforts to obtain the sacred records, Lehi's sons were stripped by Laban of all their gold, silver, and precious things. The receipt of heavenly gifts was to be accomplished in the Lord's way, by the power of His mighty arm.

How is baptism like the Rosetta Stone of spiritual experience?

Baptism is the first definitive step that we take on our journey to Christ. The path that lies beyond the font leads to the tree of life. It is not a freeway, but a toll road. Until we have paid the price, we cannot hope to comprehend with fluency the language of the Spirit that clearly explains how to make our way to the tree, that we might harvest its delicious fruit.

How can baptism unlock the gift of the interpretation of tongues?

This gift include the ability to hear the words of the prophets, and of the scriptures, with a clear and unambiguous understanding. As the Lord told Joseph Smith: "These words are not of men...but of me; wherefore, you shall testify they are of me. ...For it is my voice which speaketh them unto you; for they are given by my Spirit unto you, and by my power you can read them one to another; and save it were by my power you could not have them. Wherefore, you can testify that you have heard my voice, and know my words." (D&C 18:34-36).

How does baptism prepare us to shout praises unto the Holy One of Israel?

The commission of the missionaries who serve throughout the world is to preach the Gospel and baptize the nations. Their authority is accompanied by an endowment of priesthood power. We also remember the Nephite children whom Jesus blessed, whose tongues were loosed, and who "did speak unto their fathers great and marvelous things." (3 Nephi 26:14).

71.

We are baptized that our hearts
might be "knit together
in unity and in love."
(Mosiah 18:21).

How does baptism help us to make sense of the myriad elements of The Plan?

Baptism coherently stitches foundation principles together into an understandable pattern, so that the power of the word and the witness of truth may be conveyed without the need for external warrant.

What legacy will you leave behind when you pass through the veil?

God's design stands in contrast to the best-laid plans of mice and men that often go awry. His Plan does nothing short of preparing those on both sides of the veil to embrace eternity. Its principles illuminate activities that must be performed by the living and the dead, that all might inherit eternal life. With each step that we take, He identifies beforehand the costs required to realize our dreams. The Atonement permits us to work within time lines that are flexible enough to allow for trial and error, until "we all come in the unity of the faith, and of the knowledge of the Son of God...unto the measure of the stature of the fulness of Christ." (Ephesians 4:13).

Can eight year old children be spiritually prepared for baptism?

The Plan imposes no age restrictions for participation, other than defining the age of accountability as it relates to the need for baptism. In the Lord's Church, three year olds, thirty year olds, and ninety year olds all sing "I am a Child of God" with equal fervency.

Are there any missing elements in the pattern He has planned?

The Plan is absolutely non-discriminatory. It was designed for the world's heaviest person, who weighed in at 1,400 pounds, for the world's tallest person, at 8 feet 11 inches, the world's wealthiest person, who boasts $72 billion in assets, the world's smartest person whose I.Q. is 210, as well as for the other 7 billion of us who fall short of these extremes.

> We are baptized that we might enjoy the companionship of "the Comforter, which showeth all things, and teacheth the Peaceable things of the kingdom." (D&C 39:6).

How is baptism like a commencement exercise?

At our baptism, we matriculate into a curriculum that teaches us to become fluent in the language of the Spirit. Baptism is a part of the tuition that we pay to receive the antidote for poisonous telestial tendencies that would choke the expression of celestial sureties.

How can baptism help us to conquer our self-defeating behaviors?

Baptism clears our minds, gives us a sense of worth and of purpose, and facilitates our enjoyment of the consciousness of victory over our self-defeating behaviors. Baptism invites us to experience a holy communion with the Comforter, whose companionship allows us to conquer those telestial tendencies that would otherwise mire us in the quicksand of carnality, sensuality, and devilishness.

How can living water nurture our understanding of truth?

Living water is so crucial to our well-being that the Lord has provided the means to penetrate solid limestone, as it were, so that it may freely flow into our lives. Baptism creates a conduit that is chiseled through our rough exterior and stony nature with the tools of faith, obedience, study, prayer, good works, and other healthy lifestyle choices.

Why is faith without works dead, that it cannot save us? (See J.S.T. James 2:14)

The conduit to living water is created when we not only believe, but also act on our belief, by being honest, true, chaste, benevolent, virtuous, kind, and in doing good to others. Living water has the power to sustain our lives when we are doers, and not only hearers, of the word. (See James 1:22).

73.

> We are baptized as a witness and a testimony that we are "willing to serve God with all (our) hearts." (Mosiah 21:35).

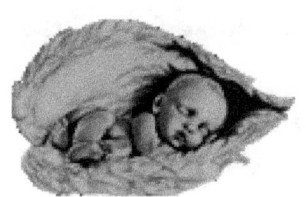

How can we fulfill our covenant to minister to the needs of others?

It permits us to listen with sensitivity and to be receptive to the cries of the downtrodden and oppressed, to see with a clarity that impels us to be responsive to the needs of our fellow travelers, and to be benevolently blind to their shortcomings.

How can witnessing for Christ update the software of His Plan?

We cannot afford to wait, if updates to the freeware of The Plan of Salvation are now available. Procrastination siphons away power that is critical to the enhancement of Heavenly Father's meticulously designed operating system. Clearing our desktop eliminates the clutter that might otherwise distract us from updating now. It helps us to avoid the spinning wheels of crisis management, first putting out one fire and then another, but never purposefully focusing our energies on the particles of our faith, that are as white hot sparks that are struck off the divine anvil of God. Bearing our testimonies invigorates our witness, and protects it from the contamination that can compromise carefully constructed code.

How can we follow the example of Aaron?

We can come unto the door of the tabernacle of the congregation, there to be washed with water. We can put on holy garments, and be anointed, and sanctified. (See Exodus 40:12-13).

What are the ordinances of salvation and exaltation?

We begin with the baptismal covenant, and then continue to make promises with Heavenly Father, culminating in those made at the altar of the temple, the fulfillment of which will bring us earthly blessings and eternal exaltation. By focusing our attention on our covenants, our thirst is quenched with the living water provided by the endowment.

74.

> We are baptized in such a manner that, as we step out of the font, our faces will always be oriented toward the light.

How can we invite the Spirit, that we might reach out and touch the face of God?

At baptismal services in particular, we feel the Spirit through the medium of music. We are reminded that even before the foundations of the earth were laid, music filled the celestial air, when "the morning stars sang together, and all the sons of God shouted for joy." (Job 38:7).

Why should we keep our faces oriented to the light? (See D&C 88:118).

As our circle of knowledge grows, so do the borders of darkness that encroach upon the edge of the light. The more we know, the more we need to learn, in order to deal with the opposition that is present in all of our undertakings. Baptism centers us, and orients us toward the light so that the shadows will always be behind us.

What can happen to us if we do not steadfastly face the light?

We walk precariously close to personality precipices when we try to negotiate the slippery slope of moral equivocation. Vice can be "a monster of so frightful mien, as to be hated needs but be seen. Yet seen too oft, familiar with her face, we first endure, then pity, then embrace." (Alexander Pope).

If we allow it to do so, where will our illuminated path lead us?

Because of our baptismal covenant, one day in the not too distant future, the atmosphere will be pungent with a heavenly aether that is punctuated by the melodious strains of our native language. Every detail will be just as we had imagined it would be, including the reassuring radiant heat of a celestial fire kindled beforehand by Father. We will know that this is just where we belong, at Home once again.

75.

> We are baptized that we might pursue the object
> and design of our existence, which is to be
> the happiest people upon the face
> of the earth.

How does baptism strengthen us on our journey to Christ?

As we feast upon the word of Christ, we will receive health in the navel and marrow in the bones, (see D&C 89:18), strength in the loins and in the sinews (see Job 40:16-17), power in the priesthood (see D&C 107:14), nourishment from the scriptures, and we will be fortified to endure to the end in righteousness, to receive the grace of God, and to enter into His Rest. (See 2 Nephi 31:20).

From Whom do our feelings of happiness come?

With our baptism comes the dawn of recognition that our opportunity for happiness is a gift that Heavenly Father weaves into every Gospel principle. When we accept the invitation to "try the virtue of the word of God" and are exposed to the fruit of the tree of life, we open our senses to a matchless realm of joy that can be ours simply by obedience to His law. (See Alma 31:5).

How do we hear the voice of the Spirit in quiet moments?

The Psalmist wrote: "Be still, and know that I am God." (Psalms 46:10). It is only when we tune out the world's cacophony of confusion, and reject the spurious coin of counterfeit currency that is proffered by moneylenders in the temple, that we sense the presence of our Heavenly Father.

What kind of spiritual nourishment is served at baptismal celebrations?

Our baptism unleashes a spiritual cornucopia. We feast upon the nourishing bread of life that has been provided, drink from a well of living water, and with renewed energy "press forward with a steadfastness in Christ, having a perfect brightness of hope, and a love of God." (2 Nephi 31:20).

> We are baptized because, as disciples
> of Christ, it is our lot in life
> to be sent forth as sheep
> in the midst of wolves.
> (See Matthew 10:16).

How can our baptism take us in the direction of our dreams?

One of life's temptations is to confuse dreams with reality, but a defeat of cosmic proportion comes when our dreams are surrendered to the narrow and confining reality of the carnal and sensual world. When that happens, life becomes nothing more than an overnight stay in a cheap hotel, in a room illuminated only by a bare 25 watt bulb dangling from a frayed cord.

How can our baptism help us to maintain order in a chaotic world?

The world may have gone mad, but the Church remains an island in the storm, and the Gospel of Jesus Christ provides a refuge from the uncertainties of life. It speaks a language of stability, direction, and purpose to those who are uncertain and hesitant. Of the Lord's children, it might be said: "The stars fade away, the sun himself grows dim with age, and nature sinks in years; But thou shalt flourish in immortal youth, unhurt amidst the war of elements, the wreck of matter, and the crash of worlds." (Joseph Addison, "Cato").

How can we exercise self-restraint following our baptism?

Those who have been baptized stand out against those with undisciplined minds who have been seduced by the siren song of Satan's sentinels. Without the stabilizing influence of the Gospel, unprincipled character will crumble in the face of telestial temptations that are tantalizing and yet traumatizing. The more our society focuses on the idols of the day, the more it will trivialize the legitimate rule of priesthood authority that administers baptism. It is this substitution of the sacred by the profane that is an abomination in the sight of God.

How can the Light of Christ protect us from the influence of the adversary?

It provides a shield of protection against the corrosive spatter of perspiration cast off by the destroyer, who is insidiously and persistently working overtime to damage our doctrinal defenses, dull our spiritual sensitivities, diminish our charitable capacity, deplete our bountiful reservoirs of sympathy, and destroy our devotions, even as we labor with an equal but opposite intensity to deify our work on the earth.

77.

*We are baptized that we might be blessed with
the means to calibrate our lives with
the pattern of heaven itself.*

How is baptism related to the Infinite Atonement?

Baptism gives all of Heavenly Father's children equal opportunity. We all "may have the privilege, living or dead, of accepting the conditions of the great Plan of Redemption provided by the Father, through the Son, before the world was." (John Taylor).

How does the Light of Christ help us to fill the measure of our creation?

The Light of Christ encourages us to examine what it means to be anxiously engaged. (See D&C 58:27). It inspires us to plumb the depths of our commitment to the Savior, and sensitizes us to the nobility of His work. It makes us more acutely aware of His grace, by bringing the visions of immortality and eternal life into focus.

How important is it to have an understanding of "the age of accountability?"

Those who teach the doctrine of infant baptism believe that children who die without the ordinance will go to hell. But the truth is that it is the professors of that doctrine who are themselves "in danger of death, hell, and an endless torment." (Moroni 8:21). The scriptures testify boldly of these things because what is at issue is an unambiguous understanding of the eternal destiny of God's precious children.

How can we experience mortality while maintaining a connection with eternity?

The entrance requirements for those who would abide the law of heaven are the same for all who have ever walked the earth. When we came from the eternal vantage point of the abode of the Gods, a resetting of our celestial chronometer was required. It is now calibrated to a temporal scale by omniscient, omnipotent, and omnipresent Beings, whereas the reckoning had been beforehand "the Lord's time, according to the reckoning of Kolob." (Abraham 3:4).

> We are baptized that the Lord might be on our right, and on our left, and in our hearts.
> (See D&C 84:88).

What mentors have accompanied you during your journey to the waters of baptism?

We realize how heavily we borrow from the towering example of those who have been our mystical mentors, our sensible chaperones, our spiritual guides, our surrogate saviors, and our compassionate critics.

As you make the journey to Christ, how can you feel His presence? (See Alma 37:41).

The Savior becomes our avatar, showing us the way, strengthening our testimonies, and teaching us humility. He is there to steady our shaking knees and nurture our faltering faith, to bind up our wounds, and to apply the Balm of Gilead to our soul scars. He provides both tangible and immaterial support, emboldens us with words of encouragement from the scriptures, and cheers us on with the wise counsel of His anointed servants.

How does the Savior work through others to guide us?

We are strengthened by a multitude of angels thinly disguised as our family and friends. We remember the words of Sir Isaac Newton, who, when pressed to reveal the great secret behind his accomplishments, simply replied: "I stood on the shoulders of giants."

How does Satan influence us to abandon the Savior as our traveling companion?

Satan has focused significant energies, and has invested immense resources, to influence us to walk alone in the dark. He goes about it by working under the radar. He creates economic burdens to get mothers out of the home and into the workplace. He employs political pressure, under the guise of "equal opportunity." Within the ivory towers of academia, he tutors the rising generation with carefully groomed mentors who are rebels without a cause, and who rail against every proven principle in the name of intellectual curiosity.

79.

We are baptized that we might more easily memorize
our lines in Heavenly Father's Three Act Play
that is entitled "The Plan of Salvation."

What kinds of distractions does Satan employ to disrupt the execution of The Plan?

Satan has a PhD (Philosophy of the Devil) in computer science, and is very good at hacking into and compromising the integrity of our operating system. His spyware not only monitors how we are using our existing software, but without our knowledge, it can also change our settings, resulting in frustratingly slow connections to sites we often visit. We might even be misdirected to sites that bear no resemblance to the one we wished to enter. Sometimes his malware creates a debilitating compromise of the functionality of the very programs that control our feelings, our attitudes, and even our basic life-support. His viruses may disguise themselves as any number of self-defeating behaviors that subtly influence us to believe that we can Restart Later.

How does our understanding of the Fall and of the Atonement provide clarity?

These doctrines liberate us from apostate teachings relating to the baptism of little children. "For awful is the wickedness to suppose that God saveth one child because of baptism, and the other must perish because he hath no baptism. Wo be unto them that shall pervert the ways of the Lord after this manner, for (after they understand the role of accountability as it relates to the fall of Adam, and understand the necessity of the Savior's Atonement) they shall perish except they repent." (Moroni 8:15-16).

How does baptism orient us toward the mysteries of eternity?

"Great and marvelous are the works of the Lord," Jacob exclaimed. "How unsearchable are the depths of the mysteries of him... And no man knoweth of his ways save it be revealed unto him." (Jacob 4:8). "O the vainness, and the frailties, and the foolishness of men!" wrote Lehi. For "when the are learned, they think they are wise" and they suppose "they know of themselves, wherefore, their wisdom is foolishness and it profiteth them not." (2 Nephi 9:28-29). As Paul cautioned the Colossian Saints: "Beware lest any man spoil you through philosophy and vain deceit, after the tradition of men, after the rudiments of the world." (Colossians 2:8).

Do you think you shouted for joy when you first heard about The Plan?

When we are baptized, we have feelings of deja vu, that when we reach out and touch the face of God, we have done so before. We vaguely remember that time when "the morning stars sang together, and all the sons of God shouted for joy." (Job 38:7).

We are baptized that we might become as lights that are set on a hill. (See Matthew 5:14).

What does it mean to magnify our callings? (See D&C 84:33).

Fulfilling the requirements of our stewardship, or magnifying our calling, means to build it up in dignity and importance, to make it honorable, to enlarge and strengthen it, and to simply perform the service that pertains to it. John Taylor taught: "If you do not magnify your calling, God will hold you responsible for those whom you might have saved, had you done your duty."

How does light manifest itself as inspiration and revelation?

One exciting element of light is the constant stream of inspiration that cascades down from above. As we walk along illuminated pathways, no individual or institution may legitimately claim or have a monopoly on divine guidance. The leveling influence of personal revelation is the great equalizer, giving each of us the same privileges to use our faculties of mind, intellect, and spirit to "come unto Christ." (Moroni 10:32).

How does the light that emanates from Christ speak to us?

As in a heavenly language that is rhythmical, melodious, soothing to our ears, and calming to our souls, when we hear the Spirit quietly whisper: "You're a stranger here," we are struck by the realization that we have "wandered from a more exalted sphere." (Eliza R. Snow).

Why is it important to always walk in the light?

Tom Paine wrote that there will be times in our lives that try our souls. Yet we will have this consolation: "The harder the conflict, the more glorious the triumph. What we obtain too cheap, we esteem too lightly; 'tis dearness only that gives everything its value. Heaven knows how to put a proper price upon its goods." ("Common Sense"). It would be strange, indeed, if such a celestial article as baptism should not be highly rated.

81.

> We are baptized that our vessels might
> be filled with the "oil of gladness."
> (See Hebrews 1:9 & Matthew 25:1).

How does the currency of faith accrue with interest, to our benefit?

As we quietly carry out our work as disciples of Christ, the righteousness of our cause will be revealed in marvelous simplicity and plainness. Walls of opposition will crumble and fall away, and the Lord will comfort and succor us with the bread of life. (See 1 Nephi 8:30).

How can the Lord go before us, and the God of Israel be our rearward? (See Isaiah 52:12).

As we travel through Idumea's harsh and unforgiving environment, oases will spring up in the deserts of life, and living water will slake our thirst because our roots have been deeply embedded in the rich loam of eternally valid principles.

How do the terms of our lease on life invite us to look with gratitude to to the Author of Salvation?

Sir Walter Scott may have been thinking of the eternal blessings related to baptism, as well as to the contrasting element of the stark reality of living month-to-month, when he wrote: "Breathes there the man, with soul so dead, who never to himself hath said, 'This is my own, my native land!' Whose heart hath ne'er within him burned, as home his footsteps he hath turned from wandering on a foreign strand!" In baptism, we find our way Home.

How does baptism protect us from going down to anonymous graves?

The poem continues: "If such there breathes, go, mark him well. For him no minstrel raptures swell. High though his titles, proud his name, boundless his wealth as wish can claim; despite those titles, power, and pelf, the wretch, concentered all in self, living, shall forfeit fair renown, and, doubly dying, shall go down to the vile dust, from whence he sprung, unwept, unhonored, and unsung." ("The Lay of The Last Minstrel"). Oh, the urgency of faith, repentance baptism, and the receipt of the Holy Ghost!

We are baptized to wash away the cobwebs from our minds.

Do those with diminished mental capacity have need to repent and be baptized?

As Moroni explained, they are not accountable, because The Plan specifically ordained that they "are alive in Christ." (Moroni 8:22). Without sin, there is no need for repentance, or for baptism. "For the power of redemption cometh on all them that have no law; wherefore...he that is under no condemnation, cannot repent; and unto such baptism availeth nothing." (Moroni 8:22).

What discoveries await us as we "walk in the light of the Lord?" (Isaiah 2:5).

We learn that in the premortal realm, we knew and worshipped our Father and accepted His Plan by which we could obtain bodies and gain experience to progress toward perfection; ultimately to realize our divine potential as heirs of eternal life. We learn that The Plan of Happiness extends its reach beyond the grave, and that sacred temple ordinances make it possible for us be reunited with our families for eternity.

What is captivating about the positive behavior changes that follow our baptism?

Baptism addresses the issues of self-denial, meekness, and charity, and asks that we surrender to the Savior our desire for self-actualization, self-renewal, self-determination, self-fulfillment, self-aggrandizement, and even self-control. It asks us to honor God's design, rather than patronizing the twisted temporal theories of emotional well-being that lack an upward thrust. It asks us to "let go and let God." In the waters of baptism, we catch a religious fever that elevates our testimony temperature enough to stir our blood with the sure knowledge of the truth. (See Alma 23:6).

How can we better understand the principles and doctrines of the Gospel?

Within the pages of The Book of Mormon, we learn that "the first fruits of repentance is baptism; and baptism cometh by faith unto the fulfilling the commandments; and the fulfilling the commandments bringeth remission of sins; and the remission of sins bringeth meekness, and lowliness of heart; and because of meekness and lowliness of heart cometh the visitation of the Holy Ghost, which Comforter filleth with hope and perfect love, which love endureth by diligence unto prayer, until the end shall come, when all the saints shall dwell with God." (Moroni 8:25-26).

> We are baptized that the anchors of our
> faith might rest within a foundation
> of rock, and not of sand.
> (See Matthew 7:26).

What are the fruits of faith? (See Alma 32:40).

For the fruits of faith to flourish, three conditions are essential. First is the recognition of a Gospel principle. Second is an understanding of the Lord's word concerning the principle, and third is experience with the principle.

What did the Savior teach the Nephites about baptism?

The Savior said: "This is the gospel which I have given unto you — that I came into the world to do the will of my Father, because my Father sent me. And my Father sent me that I might be lifted up upon the cross; and after that I had been lifted up upon the cross, that I might draw all men unto me. ...And it shall come to pass, that whoso repenteth and is baptized in my name shall be filled." (3 Nephi 27:13-20).

How can baptism help us to come to "the knowledge of the Son of God?" (Ephesians 4:13).

With our baptism, resources become available that instruct and inspire us to take advantage of the other ordinances of the Gospel. These introduce us to the three-fold mission of the Church, which is to perfect the Saints, preach the Gospel, and cement family relationships in both time and eternity. We become unified in our faith as we build each other's testimonies of the mission of the Author of Salvation.

How does baptism provide a foundation of stability?

In a world that seems to lack moral footings, what is important is that we live our lives so that every morning when we rub the sleep from our eyes, Satan exclaims: "Oh no! They're awake again!"

We are baptized that we might fan with
faith the fire of our resolve.
(See Jeremiah 20:9).

What does baptism teach us about self-reliance?

We sink or swim, largely on our own. As we persevere, we hope and pray for the serenity to accept the things we cannot change, the courage to change the things we can, and the wisdom to know the difference. But it is always nice to get a little help from our friends (including our Savior, who led the way with His own baptism). (See John 14:6).

In what ways does baptism empower us?

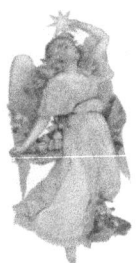

Baptism endows us with the courage to go into the world to spread the Lord's message. Through us, He invites "all to come unto him and partake of his goodness; and he denieth none that come unto him, black and white, bond and free, male and female; and he remembereth the heathen; and all are alike unto God, both Jew and Gentile." (2 Nephi 26:33). As we leave the font, we stand independent above all creatures, knowing that our sum is now the Church, and that the body to which we bear allegiance is far greater than all of its parts. Infinity, ∞ , was surely conceived with members of the Church in mind.

How can we maintain a heightened intensity of feeling after baptism?

Alma asked a penetrating question that demands our attention: "And now, behold, if ye have experienced a change of heart, and if ye have felt to sing the song of redeeming love" that you experienced at your baptism, "I would ask, can ye feel so now?" (Alma 5:26).

How can baptism help to liberate those who have been held captive by the values of the every-day world? (See Isaiah 55:9).

With the spotlight coming from above, our baptism quickens our minds and opens our hearts to spiritual realities that occupy center stage. Baptism invites us to move beyond our three-dimensional mortal experience. We look before us, behind us, and to both sides, but we also experience an upward reach that takes us into an other-worldly spiritual dimension. We look up to God, "whose brightness and glory defy all description," and in doing so, we live. (J.S.H. 1:17, see Alma 37:47).

> We are baptized that we might leave a light
> burning for those who are late to
> arrive at the wedding feast.
> (See John Chapter 2).

Who among us needs a boost, every now and then?

When life's burdens weigh us down, and slow our progress along the path that leads to the waters of baptism, whether we are professional athletes or practiced panhandlers, living in the fast or the slow lane of life, whether we have rags or riches, are leaders or lepers, are late bloomers or early prodigies, venture capitalists or welfare recipients; no matter our circumstances, if our tentative steps betray our faltering faith, we can turn to the Savior to be a bridge over troubled waters.

What is the fate of those who refuse the invitation to be baptized?

Those who do not believe in the power of God unto salvation, who will not be baptized, will not be able to continue their progression. For others, who might not be aware that the wedding feast is in progress, the foundation principles of The Plan of Salvation will have been, at least temporarily, suspended. However, the invitation has been sent out across the heavens by our Father, and He is even now waiting for their R.S.V.P.. (See D&C 123:12).

What can the children of light do to strengthen the testimonies of others?

As the congealed distillate of our life experiences, our thoughts and feelings relating to the Savior stand revealed as our innocent attempts to yoke our emotions to language. We hope that others will find our expressions of faith refreshing, will use them as food for thought, and will be motivated to act upon their expanding understanding of the principles of The Plan.

How can the universality of immortal longings be explained?

All of Heavenly Father's children are entitled to enjoy the influence of the Light of Christ. There is no scholastic prerequisite relating to The Plan of Salvation. Those without formal education are welcome to participate, as are those with advanced degrees from the most prestigious institutions of higher learning. It is the poor in spirit, however, those with broken hearts and contrite spirits, who seem to have an advantage when it comes to acting upon their immortal longings.

86.

> We are baptized that we might learn
> how to consecrate to the Lord
> our time, talents, means, and
> everything else with which
> He has blessed us.

What happens to us when our priorities are out of order?

Whenever our priorities are out of order, we lose the power to bring about positive change. Baptism, however, sharpens our perspective, enabling us to comprehend and build upon principles of perfection that are validated by the Spirit and the example of the Savior.

How does baptism provide us with opportunities to study, pray, and commit ourselves to purposeful plans of action? (See Alma 32:37).

With our baptism, we feel the word enlarge our souls and enlighten our understanding. As Brigham Young said: "Every Gospel principle carries within it a witness that it is true." It is in the economy of the Gospel that "we often catch a spark from the awakened memories of the immortal soul, which lights up our whole being as with the glory of our former home." (Joseph F. Smith).

How does baptism prepare us to more thoughtfully budget our time?

Concentrating on the things that really matter endows us with a greater capacity to manage the gift of time. We learn to take time with discipline, make time with diligence, find time with care, spend time with thoughtfulness, invest time with wisdom, and share time with pleasure.

How can we turn our attention to the weightier matters of the law?

Focusing on the things that matter most gives us a sense of independence, as we learn something new every day. Learning how to control our time can open our hearts and our minds to a breathtaking expansion of understanding. As we practice a learning style that embraces the Spirit, we discover the pattern of heaven, and it becomes our norm. (See Matthew 23:32).

87.

> We are baptized that we might accept our Heavenly
> Father's invitation to join Him in His work
> and glory, which is to bring about our
> immortality and eternal life.
> (See Moses 1:39).

How is baptism the key to our understanding of the mission statement of our Heavenly Father? (See Moses 1:39).

Whisperings of the Spirit confirm that there is more to the Gospel than outward observances, obedience, and covenants. The gift of spiritual enlightenment is the key to our discovery of undreamed vistas of otherwise inaccessible experience.

What is meant by the expression "one Lord, one faith, and (only) one baptism?" (Ephesians 4:5).

The ordinance that admits us into the fold of Christ must be carried out according to specific and pointed instruction, for except we "be born of water and of the Spirit," declared the Savior, we "cannot enter into the kingdom of God." (John 3:5).

Why is the day of our baptism such a happy occasion?

Our baptism rivets our attention on one of Heavenly Father's greatest gifts, which is the happiness that accompanies untroubled souls. As we descend into the waters of baptism, we realize that we have used our free will to choose the Savior, even as we yield our hearts to Him, ponder the great and terrible consequences of Gethsemane, and travel with Him to Calvary. We enjoy the sweetness of the redeeming power of the Atonement, which is the keystone of The Plan of Happiness. We determine to keep the laws of God. We learn to enjoy feelings that transcend temporal security and worldly comforts, described by Jacob as "that happiness which is prepared for the saints." (2 Nephi 9:43).

How can we be assured of eternal life, following our baptism?

We very quickly recognize the pathway before us that leads to spiritual transformation and a Christ-centered life. The Sacrament allows us to regularly recommit ourselves to internalize the truths and principles relating to eternal progression, and endows us with the power to endure to the end in righteousness. Some may consider these burdens of responsibility to be too heavy, but countless witnesses have testified how obedience has, for them, become the perfect law of liberty. (See James 1:25).

We are baptized that we might rejoice in our
characterization as a peculiar people.
(See 1 Peter 2:9).

How does the perfecting process of The Plan refine us? (See Malachi 3:2).

In the beginning, Heavenly Father knew that Adam would transgress the law, become mortal, and suffer physical and spiritual, death. Thus, a Savior was provided, Who was the lamb slain from the foundation of the world, that the posterity of Adam might be saved from their sins, be redeemed by the power of the Atonement, and qualify by baptism to be crowned with immortality and eternal life.

How does it feel to know that we are on the path of progression?

Christ is the Author of Salvation, (Hebrews 5:9), and the Finisher of our Faith, (Hebrews 12:2), but The Plan was introduced to His spirit children by Heavenly Father. (See 2 Nephi 9:13). By the spirit of revelation, the Holy Ghost testifies of Christ and of the Father's Plan. (D&C 8:2-3). Working in perfect harmony, the three members of the Godhead promote the Doctrine of Christ with one shared goal: to bring us by the waters of baptism to the portal of the Celestial Kingdom.

What principles do you think might have been presented at the Council in Heaven before our world was created? (See D&C 138:55).

We who were in attendance at the Council, who so readily and enthusiastically raised our arms to the square to support our Father's proposal, (see Job 38:7), must have felt the import of the moment, that our Elder Brother Jesus Christ was making history. In fact, He was creating a binding precedent to re-write history itself. We were eyewitnesses to the vitalization of "the merciful plan of the great Creator." (2 Nephi 9:6).

Do you think that baptism might have been one of the hot topics that were discussed at the Council in Heaven? (See D&C 138:56, Abraham 4:26, & 5:2).

We must have palpably sensed the enveloping reach of the Savior's love, understood His supernal example of selflessness, cherished His supreme act of sacrifice, and treasured His superlative expression of altruism. He had just become our personal Redeemer, as the power of the Infinite Atonement was activated in our behalf, only conditioned upon our baptism into His Church.

We are baptized that righteousness might
stay the sword of justice that hangs
over a wicked world.
(See Helaman 13:5).

Do you think the angels in heaven are even now taking note of our behavior?

There are no shades of grey after we have received the ordinance of baptism and our minds become "single to God." (D&C 88:68). If we try to have it both ways, our double mindedness will create intellectual and spiritual schizophrenia, for we cannot be servants of the devil while purporting to follow Christ.

Why does amending our behavior also require a change of our hearts?

Evil people can do good, but in the end their works are a blessing neither to themselves nor to those whom they pretend to serve. When their good deeds are motivated only by selfish desire, they lack the power of enrichment, and are "not counted unto (them) for righteousness." (Moroni 7:7).

How can our baptism help us to distinguish good from evil?

We particularly need the gift of discernment when dealing with the media, that does an excellent job of confusing the issues of the Last Days, by reporting fake news with straight faces. We remember the caution of Mormon, who, in a prescient glimpse of our day, wrote: "Wherefore, take heed, my beloved brethren, that ye do not judge that which is evil to be of God, or that which is good and of God to be of the devil." (Moroni 7:14).

How does the Light of Christ illuminate the path that lies before us?

Heavenly Father leaves the porch light on, for those who are both early and late to arrive at the wedding feast. It is a light that fills every corner of the universe, that was provided to be a steadily burning source of inspiration; even a beacon that would guide us safely home. But Moroni mentioned his father's counsel relating to a performance cost associated with the receipt of its blessing. Mormon had taught his son that we must "search diligently in the light of Christ." (Moroni 7:18-19).

90.

> We are baptized that others might be
> influenced to follow our Exemplar.
> (See John 14:6).

Why is it important to exercise our testimonies as often as possible?

We must venture forth out of the shadows if we want to appreciate the special familiarity that the Lord enjoys with "the children of light." (John 12:36). As we describe to others how we feel about Christ, we learn to cherish the sensations that come with increasing frequency to each of us as a result of the stirrings of those deep feelings of intimacy with the Infinite.

How does our baptism unleash the power of God within us?

When our souls have been illuminated by the burning Spirit of God, we cannot remain passive. The flickering fire of faith raises our testimony temperature and quickens our pulse as we feel an upward reach within ourselves. It sensitizes us to truth, beauty, and goodness above and beyond our own attainment.

How does God make it easier for us to witness in His name?

"All things denote there is a God, yea, even the earth, and all things that are upon the face of it witness that there is a Supreme Creator." (Alma 30:23-60). "All things bright and beautiful, all creatures great and small, all things wise and wonderful, the Lord God made them all." (Cecil Alexander).

What are some evidences of the spiritual unification of the Saints?

By their actions, new converts and well-established Church members alike echo Paul, who declared to the Romans: "We, being many, are one body in Christ." (Romans 12:5). For example, in spite of the many translations of the scriptures used by members worldwide, there is remarkably little disagreement as to their meaning. The Spirit binds us together, "to act in doctrine and principle pertaining to futurity," while allowing us to enjoy our diversity across cultural boundaries. (D&C 101:78).

91.

We are baptized that our Latter-day Saint culture might help to insulate us from worldly influences.

How powerful is the wind of doctrine?

The wind of doctrine has done a remarkable job substituting "pleasure" for "happiness" in the lexicon by making sin appear inviting and by emphasizing instant gratification in social media, on TV, in the movies, and in the print media. The wind of doctrine has shifted the focus of the world, in one generation, from Life, to Look, to People, to Us, and finally to Self.

How can we better recognize the divisive influence of winds of doctrine?

The covenant of baptism is unequivocal in the demands it puts upon the disciples of Christ. It alerts them to Satan's misdirection, that would lead them from brilliant, dazzling white, through every shade of grey, to that fathomless black which, by subtraction, is the absence of uplifting thoughts, words, deeds, principles, and doctrines.

Why do those who base their math on the winds of doctrine always end up with negative sums?

When Satan does the math, even though his equations may be clothed in impressive-looking formulas, the sums are always negative. His proofs may look good, but his students are still losers, in the end. $3 + (-4) = -1$, $4 \times 3 + (-13) = -1$, and $6/3 \times 2 - 5 = -1$. When Satan is finished with them, they are left as lifeless mannequins. They may still be clothed in costly garments and fine-twined linens, and they may continue to sport expensive accessories, but beneath it all, they are nothing more than hollow shells.

How can we face the light, so the shadows will be behind us?

In the scriptures, the first recorded words of Heavenly Father were: "Let there be light." (Genesis 1:3). His last recorded words (to date) were: "This is my beloved Son, Hear Him." (J.S.H. 1:17). These two verses are as bookends to our faith. Our own sun rises and sets on our desire to be drawn to His light, to be mesmerized by His magic, and to be baptized by His priesthood servants.

> We are baptized that we might not be
> tempted to "look back," as we flee
> from Sodom and Gomorrah.
> (See Genesis 19:16).

How important is it that one have authority to baptize?

Professors of religion often "teach for doctrines the commandments of men, having a form of godliness, (while denying) the power thereof." (J.S.H. 1:19). Creeds are an abomination in the sight of God and are corrupt when they lead His children away from the truth. Insult is added to injury when hypocrisy further perverts humanized, spiritually impotent dogma, when people do not really believe, but are only "professors" of religion who are quite comfortable living in Zion, while maintaining a summer home in Idumea.

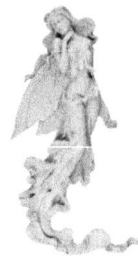

How does Satan use cunning craftiness to penetrate our defenses?

We are forewarned and forearmed because we know that he will make the most of every opportunity afforded him. He will capitalize on excessive behavior when we are over-dramatic, over-sensitive, over-bearing, over-eating, over-analytical, over-achieving, or over-whelmed. He knows that over-zealous behavior is the fast track to hell. We cannot afford to joy-ride through Babylon, stopping at its roadside attractions to satiate ourselves with their pleasures.

Why don't more people understand that one vote plus God constitutes a majority?

One vote really does count, and our destiny hangs in the balance. Ultimately, on every issue there are only three significant votes cast. Heavenly Father votes in favor of us, and Satan votes against us. Each of us casts the deciding vote as all eternity holds its collective breath and waits in hushed anticipation to see what the outcome will be. At this moment in time, we determine if we will govern our lives by priesthood principles, to find ourselves on the path leading to God's kingdom.

How can our sense of temporal security be deceiving?

With deception and a snare, Satan makes us believe that we are gaining when we are really losing. He does this by leading us by the neck "with a flaxen cord, until he (binds us) with his strong cords forever." (2 Nephi 26:22). Thus, he avoids awakening our faculties to a harsh reality. By distorting our perception, he can even twist our blessings into vehicles that amplify our feelings of self-sufficiency. Emancipation from God, however, requires us to enter into a compact with the devil.

93.

We are baptized that we might
become new creatures in Christ.
(See 2 Corinthians 5:17).

How can the scriptures expand our appreciation of the scope of The Plan?

The scriptures are little packets of light that provide refreshing illumination in a dark world.

How can baptism, and The Plan of Salvation, put us in touch with our spiritual roots?

"To use the preparation and training we receive as a springboard, to be capable of disciplined, controlled procedure and to be receptive to flashes of insight, is what solid Latter-day Saints should have going for them in their lives. The Gospel sets us free to be creative, and sets us creative to become more free. It is the perfect law of liberty." ("My Religion and Me, "Lesson #9). Truly, our baptism amplifies the quiet spiritual stirrings that underlie our mortal experience.

What does it mean to have been created in both the image and the likeness of God?

When God said: "Let us make man in our image, after our likeness," He meant not only that we should have the same physical characteristics as our Parents, but the same spiritual characteristics, as well. (Moses 2:26). Those who are like-minded seek each other out, are drawn to each other, have a natural affinity for each other, stand by each other, comfort and encourage each other, and bring out the best in each other.

How will the dead be able to accept the Gospel in the spirit world?

There is to be a thousand years of peace on the earth following the Second Coming of the Lord. During the Millennium, "Christ will reign personally upon the earth." (10th Article of Faith). Members of the Church will enjoy unimpeded access to the temples, where they will perform vicarious work for the dead. Attended by angels, they will perform the ordinances of salvation and exaltation for their ancestors, all the way back to Adam and Eve.

We are baptized that we might stand tall
for those who may lack the power
to do so themselves.

Does the Light of Christ influence all of Heavenly Father's children?

Although we must daily travel further from the East, we are nevertheless oriented toward a radiant glow emanating from that distant horizon. It provides us with the regularly recurring reassurance of a religious recalibration that auto-corrects with celestial precision. It envelops us in an intuitive appreciation of where we came from, why we are here, and where we are going. It helps us to recognize the hand of God in our affairs, and to know that there are no coincidences, but instead only an awe-inspiring divine design that has beautifully choreographed our lives.

How are those who do not understand baptism "in the gall of bitterness?" (Moroni 8:14).

Perhaps they cannot comprehend how a just and loving Father could consign so many of His innocent children to an eternal fate which, on their own merits, they did not deserve. (See Moroni 8:14). They may be "in the bonds of iniquity" because of despair regarding those who have died without baptism. (Moroni 8:14). In the end, apostate teachings leave no alternative but to suggest: "These must have gone to an endless hell." (Moroni 8:13).

How can we talk to our friends about baptism?

Even if we do not agree on every point of doctrine, we can at least agree to disagree, initiating a dialogue that leads to understanding. We can't get from A to Z without going through some intermediate steps. Perhaps this is what Isaiah meant when he urged: "Come now, and let us reason together." (Isaiah 1:18).

Why do we need to heed Paul's instruction relating to unity? (See Ephesians 2:19).

Paul compared the Saints, whether they were Ephesians, Americans, Tongans, or Utahans, to the parts of the body. Just as the head, the ears, the eyes, the nose, the mouth, the neck, the shoulders, the back, the breast, the vitals and bowels, the arms and hands, the loins, and the legs and feet are important in their different functions, so are all of those with different skills and talents who make up the sum that is the collective body of the Church.

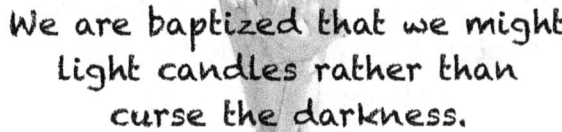

We are baptized that we might
light candles rather than
curse the darkness.

Does baptism have enough power to make a world of difference?

Every time a child of God is baptized, values are strengthened because of obedience to correct principles. The advancing tide of wickedness slows a bit, and the future looks a little brighter. A thousand points of light, when gathered together, cast a very long shadow.

Can one baptism stem the surging tide of wickedness?

Wickedness cannot be summarily eliminated, but countermeasures can be put in place to contain the problem. It is easier to hold up an umbrella than it is to turn off the rain, and it is far more effective to light a candle than it is to curse the darkness.

How can baptism prepare us for the coming millennial day?

It may be true that those who compete in the boiler room of commerce don't get what they deserve; rather, they get what they negotiate. But when the earth is cleansed to receive its paradisiacal glory, a higher standard will prevail and each of us will get exactly what we deserve. In the meantime, baptism helps us to conduct our affairs so that they reflect our joyful anticipation of that millennial day.

How does baptism put us on the path of priesthood direction?

Ultimately, each of us must ask: "Am I going to follow the prophet, or follow the profit?" "Am I going to be a Saturday Saint, a Sabbath day Saint, or a Latter-day Saint?" Priesthood direction defies spiritual Babylons' perverted concept of equality. In its attempts to be inclusive, the world does not understand that if you don't stand for something, you will fall for anything. A permissive society has, by definition, lost its orientation on the Son of God as the Master of the universe.

We are baptized that it might become easier to approach the Lord with our sacrifices.

What is the difference between a donation and a sacrifice?

A chicken and a pig were discussing plans for a potluck dinner. "I'll bring the eggs, and you provide the ham," said the chicken. The pig thought about this for a minute, and then replied, "You know, your contribution is a donation, but mine is surely a sacrifice."

How comprehensive must our sacrifice be, before it is acceptable to the Lord?

Joseph Smith said that a religion that does not require the sacrifice of all things lacks the power to save our souls. This is the essence of the Gospel of Jesus Christ. And so, it makes no difference on which principle of the Gospel we may be focusing. The distance to the Celestial Kingdom of God is measured in faith, and not in miles. It is not a question of cost, but rather of sacrifice.

What is an honest tithe?

A 1970 letter from the First Presidency stated that, notwithstanding the fact that members should pay one-tenth of their income as a tithe to the Church, "every member is entitled to make his or her own decision as to what they owe the Lord, and to make payment accordingly." (March 19, 1970). Hence, the exact amount that is paid is far less important than that each member feels that he or she has been honest with the Lord.

How is the payment of tithing a barometer of our spiritual maturity?

In 1881, obedience to the law of tithing became a requirement for temple attendance for those with an income. (J.D. 22:207-208). Payment of a full tithe, it seems, is a good barometer of our spiritual maturity, and provides an easily quantifiable way to measure our core testimony temperature.

97.

> We are baptized that we might be given
> opportunities to make and to keep
> the covenants of salvation
> and exaltation.

What was Benjamin's counsel regarding obedience to our baptismal covenant?

His ancient but apropos warning was to watch ourselves judiciously, to be the meticulous guardians of our thoughts, the scrupulous custodians of our words, and the prudent caretakers of our deeds, to fastidiously observe the commandments of God, and to continue evenly in the faith. (See Mosiah 4:30).

How does Benjamin's counsel empower us to fill the measure of our creation?

As we hesitantly inch our way through mortality, his admonition invigorates us with renewed energy, and instills in us the desire to make sacred covenants with our Heavenly Father, that the Savior might become our traveling companion.

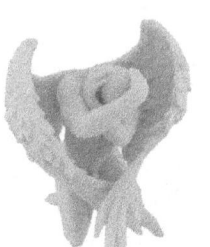

How will our witness for Christ determine our divine destiny?

Covenants force us to make choices; to be defenders of the faith or ambassadors of the adversary. In the process, all of heaven holds its collective breath, as time stands still and our fate hangs in the air as a dandelion seed caught in the summer doldrums. Covenants define us or destroy us, for they have the power to delineate our dreams, describe our destiny, and determine how, where, and with whom we will spend eternity. Covenants give us the strength to stand and give our sworn deposition before God, angels, and witnesses, thereafter to be counted among the sheep or the goats, on His right hand or His left hand.

How do covenants vitalize the work of the ministry?

Covenants bind us to to the work of the ministry, that is in turn linked to Heavenly Father's mission statement, which is to bring to pass our immortality and eternal life. (See Moses 1:39).

98.

We are baptized that we might unite
ourselves with the ordained process
by which eternal principles
are communicated.

How can others help us to "give birth" to our participation in the work of the ministry?

The Corinthian Saints had a working relationship with each other, based upon Gospel principles. Paul described their inter-connectivity in terms of their second-mile commitment: "Ye are manifestly declared to be the epistle of Christ ministered by us, written not with ink, but with the Spirit of the living God; not in tables of stone, but in fleshy tables of the heart." (2 Corinthians 3:3).

How can we make sure that our ministry does not offend people?

When we feel the urge to push His agenda, the Light of Christ can be our labor coach, providing us with just the right amount of encouragement to successfully deliver our witness of the Savior without being overbearing.

How can Heavenly Father, Jesus Christ, and the Holy Ghost infuse the universe with light?

Particle physics tells us that an incomprehensible number of photons was created at the moment of The Big Bang. The number is 1 followed by 89 zeros, which is essentially insignificant when compared to the luminosity of God. At the end of the day, "there is no power but of God." Photons have been "ordained of God" to provide reliably consistent light in a dark and dreary world. (Romans 13:1).

Is there any viable alternative to baptism?

"This is the way," Nephi said, "and there is none other way nor name given under heaven whereby man can be saved in the kingdom of God. And now, behold, this is the doctrine of Christ, and the only and true doctrine of the Father, and of the Son, and of the Holy Ghost, which is one God, without end." (2 Nephi 31:21).

> We are baptized that, henceforth, we be no more
> "carried about with every wind of doctrine."
> (Ephesians 4:14).

What are the winds of doctrine?

Winds of doctrine are those worldly influences that play mind-games with us, as they jockey for position in a competition for our attention. The stability of our baptism reminds us that we are bound in ways that bridge the cultural confusion and doctrinal dilemmas that are thrown up to hedge the way, by a world that staggers to and fro, like a drunkard. (See Job 12:25, and Psalms 107:27).

Can we avoid the consequences of sin through our own efforts?

A favorite tactic of Satan is to trick us into thinking we have all the time in the world, so that we become numb to the reality that "now is the time and the day of (our) salvation; therefore, if (we) will repent and harden not (our) hearts, immediately shall the great plan of redemption be brought about." (Alma 34:31). We must not procrastinate the day of our repentance. (See Alma 34).

How has the wind of doctrine penetrated the lives of those around us?

It is evident in the negative peer pressure that breaks down the resolve to do good. It is the silent partner of sports figures, movie stars, and other celebrities whose lifestyles reflect the vulgar tastes of the world. It substitutes the secular for the sacred, and conditions us to use words like "almighty dollar" and "movie star," so that they fall easily from our lips. It manages to substitute "notoriety" for "celebrity," so that the difference is scarcely understood.

How can baptism protect us against the power of the destroyer?

For as long as we have a work to do upon the earth, our obedience will have the effect of throwing open the windows of heaven. When the blessings of the Lord are poured out upon our heads, we will no longer "be seduced by evil spirits, or doctrines of devils, or the commandments of men." (D&C 46:7). Instead, a celestial breeze will caress our cheeks, reinvigorate our spirits, and refresh our minds with a remembrance of our former home.

100.

We are baptized that we might not be deceived "by the sleight of men, and cunning craftiness, whereby they lie in wait to deceive." (Ephesians 4:14).

What is "the sleight of men?"

There are evils and designs that exist in the hearts of conspiring men and women in the last days, that are intended to lead the righteous away from the strait and narrow way. (See D&C 89:4). The sleight of men relies heavily upon illusion, deceit, and outright dishonesty. Misdirection by the sleight of men has the potential to drive the unwary "as chaff before the wind." (Mormon 5:16).

How is the Spirit the polar opposite of cunning craftiness?

Baptismal services are blessed with the scorching holiness of God's presence, because our attention is focused on the dazzling gates of the Celestial Kingdom. For a brief moment in time, participants are refreshingly freed from the worldly reminders of the adversary that are a part of the "opposition in all things" of which Lehi spoke, and that are so much a part of our daily lives. (2 Nephi 2:11).

How can baptism offer protection from those who "lie in wait to deceive?"

With experience, we learn to recognize the tricks of their telestial trade. We guard against placing ourselves in compromising situations, because these make us more susceptible to temptation and enticements to be evil. Our covenant consciousness correctly redirects our attention to the seriousness of sin, the necessity of repentance, the power of forgiveness through the Atonement of Christ, and the blessings of heaven.

How can baptism help us to recognize the fingerprints of Satan when we are tempted by his gods of wood and stone? (See Deuteronomy 4:28).

Our covenant guards against his groping hands that have compromised and contaminated customs, culture, morals, ethics, the use of leisure time, language, and humor. He has distorted the perception of misfortune and opportunity, poverty and prosperity, adversity and privilege, and sickness and health. He has invaded the media, technology, education, health care, and sports. His influence is radioactive, mutating into unrecognizable forms the natural tendencies that have been ordained of God.

We are baptized that we might honor the order of the priesthood.

By what authority is baptism performed?

Its performance requires the authority of God, the sanction of His file leaders, exactness in its execution, and the validation of witnesses. The authority that was restored by John the Baptist will "never be taken again from the earth until," where "until" suggests a continuing sense; for example, "God be with you until we meet again." (D&C 13:1).

What was Oliver Cowdery's witness, regarding the angelic restoration of the authority to baptize?

He described the events thus: "What joy filled our hearts, and with what surprise we must have bowed...when we received under his hand the Holy Priesthood, as he said, 'Upon you my fellow-servants, in the name of Messiah, I confer this Priesthood and this authority, which shall remain upon earth, that the Sons of Levi may yet offer an offering unto the Lord in righteousness.'" (Footnote to J.S.H. 1:71).

Who are the sons of Levi that are referred to in Doctrine & Covenants Section 13?

The sons of Levi are "the sons of Moses and also the sons of Aaron (who) shall offer an acceptable offering and sacrifice in the house of the Lord." (D&C 84:31). Joseph taught that "the sons Moses and of Aaron shall be filled with the glory of the Lord, upon Mount Zion in the Lord's house, whose sons are ye." (D&C 84:32)

How can young men become the sons of Moses and of Aaron?

When they reach the appropriate age, typically ages 12 - 18, young men who remain faithful will obtain these two priesthoods and "become the sons of Moses and of Aaron, and the seed of Abraham, and the church and kingdom, and the elect of God." (D&C 84:34).

We are baptized that we might be perfected in our Savior, Jesus Christ.
(See Moroni 10:32).

How can baptism fortify us with the discipline to go the second mile?

Our spiritual awakening, though it may seem long and arduous, is acceptable to the Lord. We may take solace from the scriptures, where, although we are admonished 129 times to "learn," 154 times to be "perfect," and 407 times to "remember," we are encouraged 995 times to "begin." Thus, we read in the scriptures how "the people began to repent of their iniquity; and inasmuch as they did, the Lord did have mercy on them." (Ether 11:8).

What happens when we turn to the scriptures to learn about the Father of our spirits?

The message rings loud and clear, and resonates within our hearts: "In him we live, and move, and have our being; as certain also of your own poets have said, For we are also his offspring. (Acts 17:28). He is "the Father of all." (Ephesians 4:6). We lived with Him before we were born.

How does it make you feel to realize that Heavenly Father knows your first name?

Each of us is a child of God, known to Him by name. Although we worship together as a Church, at our baptism, and during the administration of subsequent ordinances of the priesthood, we are called by name by the officiant, who then invokes the holy name of Jesus Christ to seal the covenant promises upon our heads.

How can our baptismal covenant help us to become perfect in our repentance? (See Matthew 5:48).

Our Heavenly Father could give us everything He has, but what He is, we must earn for ourselves. The purpose of repentance is to help us to do this. As Paul asked the Hebrews: "We have had fathers of our flesh which corrected us, and we gave them reverence. Shall we not much rather be in subjection unto the Father of spirits, and live? (Hebrews 12:9). If it were not possible to become as God is, baptism, and the other principles and ordinances of the Gospel, would be unnecessary.

103.

> We are baptized that, through God's infinite goodness
> and the manifestations of the Spirit, we might have
> great views of that which is to come.
> (See Mosiah 5:3).

How can baptism help us to achieve spiritual symmetry?

Baptism orients us more to the laws of the eternal world and the guidance of the Master than to the limitations imposed by the physical world and the destructive effects of disproportion. Our experience is inexplicable, and yet undeniable. "Whatsoever is born of God overcometh the (laws governing the physical) world." (1 John 5:3).

How does baptism entitle us to further light and knowledge?

The Church provides a nurturing influence that makes it easier to have lips that have learned to articulate only positive expressions and never speak guile, shoulders that have developed the strength to bear the burdens of those who have been battered and bruised by the vicissitudes of life and who may be faltering under the heavy weight of sorrow and sin, and backs that have become sturdy enough to withstand the fierce winds of adversity and the subtle wiles of the adversary.

What does it mean to have an eternal perspective?

As Aaron taught King Lamoni's father, around a hundred years before the mortal ministry of the Savior: "Since man had fallen he could not merit anything of himself; but the sufferings and death of Christ atone for their sins, through faith and repentance, (and) he breaketh the bands of death, that the grave shall have no victory...that the sting of death should be swallowed up in the hopes of glory." (Alma 22:14).

How does Heavenly Father link baptism to the precious gift of testimony?

At our baptism, the emanation of familiar and soothing oscillations of energy resonating from within limitless reserves that are selflessly shared by the Holy Ghost will carry us along on rolling waves of the spirit toward a more sure personal witness of the Savior's divinity.

104.

> We are baptized that we might understand
> how and what we worship, that we might
> come unto our Father in the name
> of our Savior Jesus Christ.
> (See D&C 93:19).

How does baptism expose us to the mysteries of the kingdom? (See Matthew 13:11).

Our holy scriptures are called "The Standard Works" with good reason, inasmuch as the principles and doctrines contained therein are the foundation for the actions of the Lord's worldwide priesthood government, and are every member's personal "Handbook of Instructions." They are not of private interpretation. (See 2 Peter 1:20). Instead, their meaning is discerned by the Spirit that is universally accessible to those who have been endowed with the Gift of the Holy Ghost.

How does baptism free us to worship God "according to the dictates of (our) own conscience?" (11th Article of Faith).

Obedience to our covenants with God endows us with priesthood power. In fact, our salvation consists in our being placed beyond the influence of our enemies, "meaning the enemies of (our) progression, such as dishonesty, greediness, lying, immorality, and other vices." (Joseph Smith).

How do you think we felt about coming to earth, after The Plan had been fully explained to us in the pre-mortal world?

Imagine the significance of the events that were unfolding before us: The exercise of our free will had just been guaranteed, the principles of The Plan certified, the price of our future offenses successfully negotiated, and the demands of Justice satisfied and harmoniously balanced with Mercy, with a guarantee of payment made in advance. Cherubim and a flaming sword had been set in place to guard the way, in order to safeguard our opportunity to progress. Our Heavenly Father's work and glory, to bring to pass our immortality and eternal life, had been confirmed. (See Moses 1:39).

How can the ordinances of the temple become the pinnacle of our worship?

We receive living water in the House of the Lord, where we are given instruction, are endowed with power and understanding, and are promised peace and joy. We receive living water when we are washed clean from the blood and sins of this generation, through our faithfulness.

105.

> We are baptized with the realization that
> when the Lord gives us commandments, He
> also prepares ways for us to accomplish
> the tasks that are set before us.
> (See 1 Nephi 3:7).

How can sacrifice have the power to make us feel so happy?

We see what might be best for ourselves and for the Kingdom of God, develop a testimony that it should be, and then work with all our capacity to make it happen, whatever the cost might be. Then, when we are so richly blessed far beyond the measure that we deserve, the price, once paid so painfully, is recalled with gladness. We receive full value. As Brigham Young declared: "I never count the cost of anything. I just find out what the Lord wants me to do, and I do it."

How can renewing our covenant of baptism help us to lengthen our stride?

Heber J. Grant declared: "That which we persist in doing becomes easier for us. Not that the nature of the thing has changed, but our power to do is increased." Spencer W. Kimball challenged the Saints to put this concept to work, when he told the Saints: "What I am asking for is not a flashy, temporary change in performance, but a quiet resolve to lengthen our stride."

Why do you think there is a need for regular repetitive repentance?

"Whosoever repenteth and cometh unto me," said the Lord, "the same is my church. Whosoever declareth more or less than this, the same is not of me, but is against me; therefore he is not of my church." (D&C 10:67-68). Since the day the Church was organized on April 6, 1830, this doctrine has not changed. It has been taught without modification since the Restoration of the Gospel began on that date.

How can angels from heaven help us to repent?

Angels, who are the servants of Christ, are commissioned to the work. "And the office of their ministry is to call men unto repentance, and to fulfil and to do the work of the covenants of the Father, which he hath made unto the children of men, to prepare the way among the children of men, by declaring the word of Christ unto the chosen vessels of the Lord, that they may bear testimony of him." (Moroni 7:31).

106.

> We are baptized to make it easier for us to "pray unto the Lord, (to) call upon his holy name, (and to) make known his wonderful works among the people."
> (D&C 65:4).

What is our greatest joy, when we sacrifice for the kingdom?

We are, and will forever be, His junior partners, and never His equals, but we still know what it feels like to be in business with God. When we work hard, and the sweat drips off the ends of our noses, we thank our Father in Heaven for the capacity to work, for the blessing it is to feel physically fatigued, and for whatever talents we have been able to muster, to be put to use for the benefit of the Church and kingdom.

How can we keep our blessings in perspective?

When we survey the fruits of our labors, we try to envision the purpose for which we have received our blessings. If our talents are multiplied, our greatest enjoyment comes when they are put to use for the benefit of others. Our happiness is like a butterfly. The more we chase it, the more it eludes us. But when we exert ourselves in service to others, happiness comes and rests quietly on our shoulder.

What is one of the best ways to follow the Savior's example of missionary work?

As Nephi asked: "Wherefore, my beloved brethren, can we follow Jesus save we shall be willing to keep the commandments of the Father? And the Father said: Repent ye, repent ye, and be baptized in the name of my Beloved Son." (2 Nephi 31:10-11).

Can there be a greater witness than the Holy Ghost?

The witness of the Holy Ghost is "unimpeachable." It is beyond doubt, unquestioned, impervious to criticism, and entirely trustworthy. It is sometimes frustrating for the Saints to bear witness to those who have not prepared themselves to receive spiritual gifts. (See Moroni 10:4). The Savior taught that "the wind bloweth where it listeth, and thou hearest the sound thereof, but canst not tell whence it cometh, and whither it goeth. So is every one that is born of the Spirit." (John 3:8).

107.

> We are baptized so that, although we were an hungered,
> and thirsty, and strangers, we will no longer be
> naked, or sick, or imprisoned within the
> fortress of our own limiting beliefs.
> (See Matthew 25:34-40).

How does baptism help us to break free of our self-imposed limitations?

Baptism casts us upon an altar of faith whose foundation is buttressed by a supernal display of divine direction. We are driven relentlessly forward with an unwavering confidence that His power to save has been unleashed in our behalf. We feel His grace wash over our wounds as a healing balm that soothes our spirits and prepares us to unflinchingly meet His penetrating gaze.

How can baptism counteract the fading light of limiting beliefs?

Fading light is the consequence of the corrosive nature of sin, or even of the opposition in all things that is a necessary part of our mortal experience. Without baptism, which is the lynchpin of The Plan of Salvation, all must be lost. Fortunately, the Lord reveals truth to those who are spiritually prepared to embrace it, and from the beginning, has provided a pathway to perfection that all might humble themselves as little children.

How was Naaman the Leper a prisoner of limiting beliefs?

The waters of baptism are a ready invitation to those who are humble, meek, poor in spirit, and pure in heart. When Elisha directed Naaman to wash in the River Jordan seven times in order to be cured of his leprosy, this proud captain of the host of the King of Syria at first refused. But "his servant came near, and spake unto him, and said, My father, if the prophet had bid thee do some great thing, wouldest thou not have done it? How much rather then, when he saith to thee, Wash, and be clean?" Then, with the faith of a little child, "he went down, and dipped himself seven times in Jordan...and his flesh came again like unto the flesh of a little child, and he was clean." (2 Kings 5:13-14).

How can baptism liberate us from captivity?

The Law of Witnesses enjoys its most profound expression at baptismal services, for "the testimony of two men is true." (John 8:17). Witnesses link arms with the unimpeachable witness of the Holy Ghost to create a shield wall and confirm the validity of the ordinances.

> We are baptized that, with uplifted hands
> unto the Most High, our incomings, our
> outgoings, and our salutations might
> be in the name of the Lord.
> (See D&C 109:9).

How can witnesses help those who are struggling as they make the journey to Christ?

Witnessess nudge those who are groping in darkness to move closer to the Light. Jeremiah exhorted the spiritually blind and deaf inhabitants of Jerusalem: "Hear now this, O foolish people, and without understanding; which have eyes, and see not; which have ears, and hear not." (Jeremiah 5:21).

How does the Light of Christ work tirelessly to encourage us to praise God?

The Light of Christ encourages us to ponder and pray, rather than wander and play. It inspires us to walk in the light of the Lord, "lest (we) enter into temptation and lose (our) reward." (D&C 31:12, see Isaiah 2:5). It emboldens us to rely upon the revealed word of God to gain an appreciation of both the physical world and its spiritual equivalents, and even "to know the mysteries of the kingdom." (D&C 42:65).

How can the Light of Christ prompt us to lift up our hands and praise God?

The Light of Christ will not lead us to develop faith in that which is not true. It will shield us from the false teaching that the power by which the Church operates can be usurped, without the aid of revelation, by professors who purport to be the Lord's earthly representatives. It will protect us from a priesthood that believes that office automatically bestows grace without the need for the powers of heaven to legitimize authority or position.

How is baptism a re-affirmation of our pre-mortal acceptance of The Plan?

In the pre-mortal realm, as spirit sons and daughters of God, we knew and worshipped Him as our Eternal Father, and accepted His Plan by which we could obtain physical bodies and gain earthly experience to progress toward individual perfection. Thereby, we could ultimately realize our divine destiny as rightful heirs of eternal life. (See Abraham 1:2).

109.

> We are baptized that we might find
> greater happiness, peace, and rest; that we
> might obtain the blessings of the fathers,
> including the authority to administer
> the ordinances of the Gospel.
> (See Abraham 1:2).

After the close of the Savior's ministry, how successful was the Church in maintaining strict obedience to the Doctrine of Christ?

During the Age of Chivalry, Charlemagne urged his churchmen to faithful Gospel scholarship. "In a letter to abbots and bishops, he complained of illiterate monks. 'What pious devotion had faithfully prompted their hearts, their uneducated tongues could not put into words without stumbling.' Hardly a Bible existed that was not riddled with the gross errors of untutored copyists." (Will Durant).

How did the Reformation pave the way for the Restoration of the Gospel?

A leader of the Reformation in America wrote: "There is no regularly constituted Church on earth, nor any person authorized to administer any Church ordinance (such as baptism); nor can there be until new apostles are sent by the Great Head of the Church, for Whose Coming I am seeking." (Roger Williams).

What did Thomas Jefferson mean by "Primitive Christianity?"

Thomas Jefferson fumed that "the religion builders have so distorted and deformed the doctrines of Jesus, so muffled them in mysticisms, fancies and falsehoods, have caricatured them into forms so inconceivable, as to shock reasonable thinkers. Happy in the prospect of a restoration of primitive Christianity, I must leave to younger persons to encounter and lop off the false branches which have been engrafted into it by the mythologists of the middle and modern ages." ("Jefferson's Complete Works," 7:210).

How is baptism related to the Restoration of the Gospel?

The Restoration re-established the authority to act in obedience to the law of heaven. As the Savior taught: "This is the Gospel which I have given unto you – that I came into the world to do the will of my Father, because my Father sent me.... And it shall come to pass, that whoso repenteth and is baptized in my name shall be filled." (3 Nephi 27:13-20).

> We are baptized to become more
> observant followers of righteousness,
> to possess greater knowledge, to be the
> progenitors of nations and ambassadors
> of peace, and to receive instruction,
> and keep the commandments.
> (See Abraham 1:2).

Can the Church sustain true doctrine without continual revelation?

Paul had prophesied of the coming apostasy from the faith. He wrote to the Thessalonian Saints: "Be not soon shaken in mind, or be troubled, neither by spirit, nor by word, nor by letter as from us, as that the day of Christ is at hand. Let no man deceive you by any means. For that day shall not come, except there come a falling away first." (2 Thessalonians 2:2-3).

What did early Church historians have to say about apostasy from the truth?

In the third century A.D., the Church Historian Eusebius provided a glimpse of the falling away that had been spoken of by Paul. He wrote: "But with our greater freedom a change came over us. We yielded to pride and sloth. We yielded to mutual envy and abuse. We warred upon ourselves as occasion offered, and we used the weapons and the spears of words. Leaders fought with leaders, and laity formed factions against laity. Unspeakable hypocrisy and dissimulation traveled to the farthest limits of evil." ("The Essential Eusebius," p. 177).

Why did the Pharisees of His day remain silent when Jesus was baptized?

"The fact that baptism was practiced in ancient Israel might explain why the Savior was not criticized by the orthodox Jews when He was baptized. The Pharisees were quick to (rebuke) Him whenever He did anything contrary to their law. However, not a single word of criticism concerning the baptism of Jesus Christ is found in the New Testament." ("Commentary on The Book of Mormon" p. 155).

How can baptism help us to be more observant followers of righteousness?

Heavenly Father has ordained a Plan that is all the more beautiful because of its simplicity It is clearly established in the Bible and clarified in companion scriptures. It has been carefully articulated in both The Book of Mormon and the Doctrine and Covenants, in order to silence disputations among the people concerning its vital points of doctrine.

111.

> We are baptized that we might become kings and
> priests, and queens and priestesses; in effect,
> to become rightful heirs of the blessings
> that belonged to the fathers.
> (See Abraham 1:2).

Why are we baptized individually, and not in large groups?

Heavenly Father purposely designed baptism so that each time the ordinance would be performed, it would be unique, and in its own special way particularly adapted to the child of God who was then entering the fold. Thus, it is at baptismal services that we "hear truth spoken with clarity and freshness, uncolored and untranslated. It speaks from within ourselves in a language original but inarticulate, heard only with the soul." (Hugh B. Brown).

What is the eternal destiny of those who die without baptism before they reach the age of accountability?

The breath of fresh air of Latter-day revelation is unequivocal: "Children who die before they arrive at the years of accountability are saved in the Celestial Kingdom of heaven." (D&C 137:10).

To whom do the blessings of the Abrahamic Covenant apply?

Our inter-connections are solidified with service, particularly when it is directed toward those who cannot provide of their own means to generate equivalent links. Service in the temple comes to mind. In the ordinances performed by patrons there, the expression "for and in behalf of" is repetitively used. Temple ordinances give substance to the expression that "no man is an island." The Designer of The Plan created opportunities for us to perform vicarious work, that we might comfortably surround ourselves by associations with both the living and the dead, as we establish bonds between ourselves and our kindred dead whose eternal identity has been strengthened by covenants made in The House of The Lord.

Where does the pathway lead that begins with baptism?

The pathway to the Celestial Kingdom is illuminated by the principles of true conversion that point us in the direction of a clear recognition of iniquity, and then to a deep godly sorrow for our sins. Next comes inescapable suffering and torment that stimulates an appeal to the Savior, together with our awakening understanding of the power of the Atonement. From Him, comes forgiveness, spiritual enlightenment, and great joy. This motivates us to a lifestyle of righteousness and service. Each time this happens, the endless loop cycles one more time, re-calibrated to an ever higher plane.

112.

We are baptized because we have brought
forth fruit worthy of repentance.
(See Moroni 6:1).

How does baptism free us from the natural process of entropy?

Everything that is of a temporal nature gradually declines into disorder, but when we are "born of God," our orientation is more toward the expansive laws of the eternal world than to the restrictive and narrowing confines of the physical world. When we are in harmony with the eternities, we are simply in a better state of balance. We overcome the world with a freedom from incarceration to the inexorable immutability of physical laws that govern the temporal world in which we now live. (See 1 John 5:3).

Why do you think baptism has been described as a "narrow gate?" (2 Nephi 33:9).

It can be challenging to muster faith unto repentance that leads us to the strait and narrow gate of baptism. In fact, "few there be that find it." (Matthew 7:14). Those who ultimately pass through its portal will find that the way opens up before them because it is clearly marked by the Atonement of Christ.

Why do faith and repentance precede baptism? (See the 4th Article of Faith).

Baptism is the pinnacle of our experience, when through the Atonement of Christ we are liberated by independence from the bondage to sin. This feeling is incalculable, indescribable, and inexplicable, and yet it is undeniable. It is not maturational, but is generational, as we become new creatures in Christ.

When we repent, what happens to the recollection of our former sins?

Regarding sins for which we have repented, we will remember them only insofar as they increase our testimonies and strengthen our resolve to refrain from repeating them, but we will no longer bear the guilt associated with the transgression. The Spirit of the Lord Omnipotent will cause a mighty change to come over us, clearing our minds and lifting our spirits with such refreshment "that we have no more disposition to do evil, but to do good continually." (Mosiah 5:2).

113.

> We are baptized that we might give
> away all of our sins, but there
> are strings attached.
> (See Alma 22:18).

What happens when we give away our sins?

With baptism, we realize that "life is a sheet of paper white where each of us may write a line or two, and then comes night. Greatly begin. If thou hast time but for a line, make that sublime. Not failure, but low aim is crime." (James Russell Lowell).

Why do you think we take the Sacrament after our baptism?

Without the sustained nourishment that is repetitively provided by the ordinance of the Sacrament, it is inevitable that we would, sooner or later, die of spiritual starvation. (See Romans 8:13).

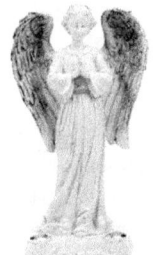

Could we be happy living in eternity if we had not given away our sins?

Though our sins "be as scarlet, they shall be as white as snow; though they be red like crimson, they shall be as wool." (Isaiah 1:18). The divine Plan of Happiness enables family relationships to be perpetuated beyond the grave. Sacred ordinances, beginning with baptism and culminating in the covenants of the temple, make it possible for God's children to return to His presence in a state of purity and innocence, and for families to be united eternally.

Who might be willing to take responsibility for our sins?

One reason the scope of the Atonement is so hard for even the disciples of Christ to grasp is that it was conceived in heaven. It is not of this world, and so if we try to wrap our finite minds around it, we will fail. But it must not be summarily dismissed just because it cannot be rationally explained. "The things which some men esteem to be of great worth...others set at naught." (1 Nephi 19:7). The Atonement is one of the mysteries of the kingdom that can only be spiritually discerned. (See 1 Corinthians 2:14). Baptism is the Lord's way to strengthen our understanding of the Atonement.

114.

We are baptized when charity has become the foundation of our faith.

How can we protect ourselves with a shield of faith?

Baptism fortifies us with the latter-day equivalent of the Hoplite phalanx of ancient Greece, the Roman testudo, and the medieval shield-wall famously employed by the Saxons at Hastings. In the case of baptism, however, participants enjoy the added protection of a shield of faith that was anciently envisioned by the Apostle Paul. He knew that the Saints would need to defend themselves against the fiery darts of the adversary with a spiritual innovation that would exceed that of the most inventive minds of the best military strategists of the ages. (See Ephesians 6:16).

Why do we sometimes feel that we fight our battles alone?

We need our shield of faith as never before, because Satan has infiltrated government, and has suppressed the will of the silent majority by legitimizing the wild, rabid, and morally indefensible demands of the vocal minority. He has snuffed out freedom of expression within democracy, and with gold and silver he has purchased armies and navies, false priests who oppress, and tyrants with whom he goes about sowing destruction upon the earth. (See Mosiah 7:31).

How can charity strengthen our shield of faith?

Baptism inspires us to be benevolently blind as we direct our charity toward others. The covenant fosters empathy, and teaches us to be less concerned with telestial trivia and more focused on celestial sureties. It gently encourages us to be humble and selfless, to be forbearing, and to reflect poise under provocation.

How are those who have been baptized strengthened to bear a shield of faith?

Those who have been baptized think no evil, have no secret agenda, and rejoice not in iniquity, but are instead repulsed by sin. They revel in the truth, believe all things, hope all things, endure many things, and hope to be able to endure all things. They are drawn to light, and are continually open to that which is uplifting. (See Moroni 7:45).

115.

> We are baptized because we have determined to follow the Savior "with full purpose of heart, acting no hypocrisy and no deception before God." (2 Nephi 31:13).

How is our discipleship vitalized when our hearts are single to God's glory?

We follow the Savior when we build up our stewardship responsibilities in dignity and importance, make them honorable and commendable in the eyes of all, enlarge and strengthen them, and simply perform the service that pertains to them. If we do not magnify our callings, God will hold us responsible for those whom we might have saved, had we done our duty.

How can we give birth to our witness of Jesus Christ?

Witnessing for the Savior is an exercise in midwifery. It is a validation of the inspiring and yet arduous process of the birth of our testimonies.

Why do you think people sometimes act with deception before God?

Perhaps they are embarrassed to be identified as Christians. But those who are baptized are "not ashamed of the Gospel of Christ, for it is the power of God unto salvation to every one that believeth." (Romans 1:16).

How can we make sure our witness is borne with full purpose of heart?

When we feel the urge to push His agenda, Heavenly Father has provided us with the Light of Christ to be our labor coach, providing us with just the right amount of encouragement to successfully deliver our witness without being overbearing.

We are baptized that we might experience liberation from our self-defeating behaviors.

How does baptism prepare us for our magnum opus in the theater of life?

Baptism invites inspiration from heaven. For example, we cannot just determine to be charitable. We need the guidance of the Spirit to lead us to those in need. In doing so, we are doubly blessed.

Why are the principles of the Gospel called "the perfect law of liberty?" (James 1:25).

We obtain our freedom from bondage to sin when we "listen to him who is the advocate with the Father, who is pleading (our) cause." (D&C 45:3). The term "advocate" is found just once in the New Testament, and is from the Greek word for "comforter." (See 1 John 2:1). Because of our obedience to the principles of The Plan of Salvation, and in particular because of our reliance upon the Atonement, the Savior becomes the father of our spiritual regeneration. The perfect law of liberty sets us free to reach our potential as the children of God.

How does baptism re-introduce us to the program of the Three Act Play that was imprinted within our subconscious minds before we came to earth?

Baptism invites us to focus on the things that matter, as we scurry about during Act Two of life's Three Act Play that is entitled The Plan of Salvation. The Holy Ghost massages us with memories of Act One, and tantalizes us with a foretaste of the wonders that await us when the inevitable curtain call signals the commencement of Act Three.

How does baptism brings out the best in us?

Our baptism prepares us to rise to the occasion, and to meet every challenge of mortality. As Mormon said: "I judge better things of you, for I judge that ye have faith in Christ." (Moroni 7:39). He was like wise old Tevya in The Fiddler on The Roof, who told his daughters: "In Anatevka, God knows who you are, and what you may become."

117.

> We are baptized that we might press forward
> with steadfastness, having a perfect brightness
> of hope and a love of God and of our brothers
> and sisters, feasting upon the scriptures, and
> enduring to the end in righteousness.
> (See Nephi 31:20).

How can the Sacrament, in its repetition, become a powerful vehicle for our personal growth?

At baptism, we are called by our user name, and then, as we participate in the ordinances of the temple, we are given the passwords that grant us access to our Heavenly Father's full database of knowledge. This endows us with a perfect brightness of hope, and a love of God and of all men, as we feast upon the words of Christ, and endure to the end in righteousness. (See 1 Nephi 31:20).

How did Joseph Smith feast upon the word of God after reading James 1:2-3?

The word of God led him to the Sacred Grove, where he learned that the creeds of Christendom were an abomination." (J.S.H. 1:19). Organizations or teachings that do not lead us clearly and directly toward salvation and exaltation in the Celestial Kingdom are abominable in the sight of God. It was this confusion and Joseph's prescient sense of impending condemnation that drove him to his knees, and introduced the world to the Dispensation of The Fullness of Times.

Why was Joseph Smith's receipt of the gift of the ministering of angels so remarkable?

His account of the initial appearance of the Angel Moroni is unique. (See J.S.H. 1:29-43). Joseph wrote that, late one evening, a light started to appear in his bed chamber, and grew brighter and brighter, until it was lighter than at noonday. Suddenly the Angel Moroni appeared before him, standing in the air. Clearly, He did not come through the door when he entered the room. He just "appeared," as if coming through a portal from another world.

How does our baptism become a commencement exercise?

Our baptism can catalyze our resolve, that our experience might be as it was on the Day of Pentecost, when the words of Peter and the other apostles carried the day by penetrating the hearts of their listeners, who were prompted to ask: "Men and brethren, what shall we do? Then Peter said unto them, Repent, and be baptized every one of you in the name of Jesus Christ for the remission of sins, and ye shall receive the gift of the Holy Ghost." (Acts 2:37-38).

We are baptized that we might hear the voice of the Lord that is unto all, for "there is none to escape; and there is no eye that shall not see, neither ear that shall not hear, neither heart that shall not be penetrated."
(D&C 1:2).

How does the Savior ask us to follow Him, both figuratively and literally?

The Savior's example demonstrates that entrance into the Church and Kingdom is strait, that is to say, it is narrowly defined. There should be no discussion or variance of opinion regarding the prescribed way. He set the pattern by commanding the children of men to follow Him. (See 2 Nephi 31:10).

How can we follow the Savior by listening to the counsel of His prophets?

Their ecclesiastical responsibility has always been to invite less active members of the Church to return to the fold in full fellowship. This was powerfully demonstrated in Russel M. Nelson's first address in 2018, as President of the Church.

How can we follow the Savior if there is confusion regarding the correct administration of the ordinance of baptism?

The history of post-apostolic Christianity illustrates the misunderstanding that has taken place concerning the Doctrine of Christ. This was presaged by the Savior's instruction to the Nephites: "And there shall be no disputations among you, as there have hitherto been. Neither shall there be disputations among you concerning the points of my doctrine." (3 Nephi 11:28).

How does the baptismal prayer in The Book of Mormon help us to follow the Savior?

Anciently, Christ gave the Nephite Twelve the specific words that they were to employ in the baptismal prayer, so that there might be no misunderstanding. (See 3 Nephi 11:22-27). Because this prayer authorizes the officiant to invoke the holy names of all three members of the Godhead, its words convey power, and suggest without reservation the sanction and approval of God Himself.

119.

We are baptized that we might affirm our support of family values.

Why are the prophets as "lone voices crying in the wilderness?" (Mark 1:3).

Our hearts are the birth-place of feeling, the center of bodily power, the focus of our rational and emotional nature, the repository of moral life, and the very hearth-stone of our impulses, where our goals and aspirations are warmed and nurtured toward ultimate expression. Unfortunately, it is often the nature of men to harden their hearts. The prophets echo the warning: "Go ye out from among the nations, even from Babylon, from the midst of wickedness, which is spiritual Babylon," a representation of sin, ungodliness, idolatry, evil, and worldliness, and a symbol of the stony hearts of those who are physically and spiritual enslaved. (D&C 133:14).

How can we fortify ourselves with the words of the prophets?

Truly, the Word is more powerful than the sword. The counsel of the prophets resonates with truth because it strikes familiar chords within us, allowing us to more easily identify the smeared fingerprints of Satan on the idols of wood and stone with which he continually tempts us. How wonderful it is to receive the gifts of the Spirit, recognize the voice of our Master, and build up our strength to resist evil as we obey His teachings. (See John 10:27).

How are we empowered to act upon the principles contained in The Proclamation on The Family?

Baptism allows our efforts to be directed toward our families, which are the basic building blocks of eternity. Our baptismal covenant teaches us to be less concerned with telestial trivia, and to be more focused on celestial sureties. It trains us to reflect poise under provocation, even as Satan loudly and insistently argues his case before the world court of public opinion.

How can baptism protect our family memories from becoming tarnished?

"My father focuses heart-gripping flashes across the wall screen. Family slides. I am small, my brother is smaller, my sister is smallest. Days now dead re-open like old storybooks from memory's heaped box. Pulling out pictures of cooking in grandfather's dutch oven; playing cheetah on our backyard monkey-jungle; being beautifully Easter-bested with my coat buttoned wrong; hugging a mommy minus grey hair. Soberly, I think of another Father, Who someday shall open my mind, and flash reeling remembering of every day's minute across my soul, across the heavens, and kindly ask me to narrate." (Lora Lyn Stucker).

We are baptized that we might become saviors on Mount Zion to our kindred dead. (See Obadiah 1:2).

How does vicarious work for the dead harmonize with the principles of The Plan?

Work for our dead in the House of the Lord harmonizes perfectly with the doctrine that God is no respecter of persons, (see Acts 10:34), that He esteems all flesh as one, (see 1 Nephi 17:35), and that He views all of His children as living. (See Job 33:4). Vicarious work for the dead is an inspired program to knit our eternal families together with the light and knowledge that are received by the power of the Holy Ghost on both sides of the veil.

How can all of Heavenly Father's children have equal opportunity to become heirs of salvation and eternal life?

"Those who did not have the opportunity to hear the message of salvation in this life, but who would have accepted it with all their hearts if such an opportunity had come to them, are the ones who will accept it in the spirit world. They are the ones for whom we shall perform the ordinances in the temple." (Joseph Fielding Smith, Jr.).

How does baptism for the dead stand beside the Atonement as a vicarious work?

Baptism for the dead is "one of the grand principles of truth revealed through the Prophet Joseph Smith." Obedience allows us to "rejoice in the kingdom of God with our relatives and friends in the reunion and assemblage of the Saints of the Church of The Firstborn." (Joseph Fielding Smith, Jr.).

How is baptism for the dead the "most glorious of all subjects belonging to the everlasting gospel." (D&C 128:17).

It is so important, that resurrected beings will help the Saints during the Millennium to complete the vicarious work of salvation. They "will help us correct the mistakes we have made in doing research concerning our dead ancestors. They will also help us find the information we need to complete our records" all the way back to Father Adam and Mother Eve. (Joseph Fielding Smith, Jr.).

121.

We are baptized that the Spirit might find expression as a light within each of us.

What will be the outcome of the battle raging in the hearts of men, on Saturday?

Conditions have not yet deteriorated so far that the wicked cannot still be recommended unto God by the priesthood servants of God. (See Mormon 7:21). In fact, Joseph Fielding Smith once declared: "I believe there has never been a moment of time since the creation but what there has been someone holding the priesthood on the earth to hold Satan in check," that the wicked, not to mention the righteous, might be spared.

Why is it important for us to maintain our unique personality signatures?

If Satan can succeed in reducing our distinctive personality signatures to the lowest common denominator, he will destroy us. If we surrender the traits that make us unique, we will fade into a shadow and a caricature of what we could have otherwise been.

How does baptism help us to regain and retain our spiritual identities?

When we have paid the price to regain our spiritual identity, we feel liberated. We enjoy the Light of Christ, and the guidance of the Holy Ghost expresses itself through our love of God and our fellowmen.

What can happen if we decline to embrace baptism's spiritual protection?

If Satan can breach the firewalls of our spiritual security system and neutralize our defense mechanisms, he will move quickly to insert his infectious virus into the perfect program written by the finger of God. The deleterious effects of his contamination of the stability, order, and direction of The Plan will be compromise, conflict, and chaos.

122.

We are baptized that Heavenly Father
might show us our weaknesses.
(See Ether 12:27).

How can our weakness be transformed into a source of strength?

Weakness can be a primer on midwifery when it germinates the arduous process of the birth of our testimonies. Confronting and dealing with weakness by relying upon the power of the Atonement enables us to bear our witness with conviction, when the questions are posed: "What think ye of Christ?" and "Whose son is he?" (Matthew 22:42).

How does the grace of God help us to deal with our imperfections?

"My grace is sufficient for all men that humble themselves before me; for if they humble themselves before me, and have faith in me, then will I make weak things become strong unto them." (Ether 12:27).

Why would Heavenly Father think to bless us with weaknesses?

Weakness can seed the atmosphere of our inspiration, prompting nurturing moisture to fall upon our tender testimonies, and facilitating the germination of the seeds of faith that are key to the transformation of our nature. When it is linked to faith, weakness can motivate us to respond to the invitation to do better and to be kinder, and to be more merciful and forgiving.

How can weakness promote the principle of progression?

Our progression hinges largely upon what do we do with our weaknesses, and what our weaknesses do for us. We may allow weakness to either impede or facilitate our progress. We are fortunate, indeed, if baptism intervenes, and laces our weakness with healthy measures of meekness and humility, in order to amend our narrow perspective, so that we might see supposed stumbling blocks as the very stepping stones that are needed to reinforce our confidence, conquer our fears, and overcome the obstacles to our progression.

123.

We are baptized that we might know
that we are here, at this place, and
in this time, by divine design.
(See 2 Nephi 2:24).

How can all things give us experience, and be for our good? (See D&C 122:7).

The culture medium of our experience is provided by our Heavenly Father as a rich agar to nourish us, as we work out our salvation with fear and trembling. (See Philippians 2:12).

How would you describe the choreography of The Plan of Salvation?

The talents of the best choreographers of music and dance are recognized with Tony Awards. However, their gifts would need to be infinitely multiplied for us to even begin to understand the awesome creative aptitude of the Architect of our salvation.

How can The Plan of Salvation be infinite in its scope, and yet be so personalized that it meets our individual needs?

There are no coincidences. There are only innumerable examples of the Lord working behind the scenes on our behalf. Everything happens by divine design.

What are divine accoutrements?

Sometimes, it seems that we only accessorize our lives with Gospel principles, rather than incorporating them into the core of our existence and experience. We must take care that we do not adorn ourselves with fine-twined linen at the cost of the full armor of God. Flaxen cords around our necks far too easily, and far too carelessly, can be transformed into heavy chains that are fastened to millstones. (See 2 Nephi 26:22).

124.

> We are baptized that we might honor God and feel His love, as we confess His hand in all things, and obey His commandments.
> (See D&C 59:21).

How does your faith compare to that of those whom Peter taught? (See Acts 2:37).

As the Restoration continues to unfold, there is a Pentecostal outpouring of the Spirit, and humble petitioners with a sincere desire to understand the will of God ask: "Now that we have heard Heavenly Father's message, and have put it to the test of prayerful inquiry, what shall we do?" Their demonstration of faith leads to the waters of baptism, with continuing commitment, dedicated discipleship, selfless service, and sustained spirituality.

How is Moroni a prototype of those who will one day be enveloped in light?

At the conclusion of Moroni's visit to Joseph Smith in his bedchamber, the light began to gather up around him, whereupon he ascended in a conduit right into heaven. One day, light may very well gather around each of us in a similar manner, as the physical confines of our mortal clay evaporate, and we return to our Maker as pure energy, trailing clouds of glory as we go.

How can baptism become the mortar that binds foundation principles together?

Jesus Christ is the Architect of the cosmos, including the "Pillars of Creation," elephant trunks of interstellar gas and dust in the Eagle Nebula, 7,000 light years from Earth. In an 1857 sermon entitled "The Condescension of Christ," London pastor Charles Spurgeon used the phrase to describe both the physical world and the force stemming from the divine that binds it all together. "Now wonder, ye angels," Spurgeon wrote of the birth of Christ, "the Infinite has become an infant. He, upon whose shoulders the universe doth hang, nurses at his mother's breast; He who created all things, and bears up the pillars of creation!"

How can the Holy Ghost help us to honor our baptismal covenant?

All that is true comes to us by the Holy Ghost. The creative drive that has guided the children of our Heavenly Father since the dawn of history can be traced back to the Holy Ghost. We constantly benefit from that which is revealed by the Holy Ghost. In the Last Days, as more of the children of God are baptized, we see in their conversion that the Spirit is being "poured out upon all flesh," as "young men see visions, and old men dream dreams." (Joel 2:28). Our baptism acknowledges the Source of that inspiration.

125.

> We are baptized to remind ourselves that
> the poor, the unlearned, the common
> person, and the native born, may
> equally come unto Christ.
> (See Acts 10:24).

Why do our experiences sometimes build us up, while at other times they seem to tear us down?

Paul exhorted the Saints to remain steadfast, in no matter what circumstances they might find themselves, no matter what cards they might be dealt in life, no matter in what twist of fate they might think themselves trapped. For, ultimately, all things would be theirs, for they were "Christ's, and Christ is God's." (1 Corinthians 3:21-23).

How does the Gospel exert a nurturing influence?

The Gospel is designed to generate enthusiasm. Its teachings create confidence, and rather than assigning blame, they show how to fix mistakes. Its doctrines and principles define authority, but delegate responsibility. Its Author, the Carpenter of Nazareth, knew how, but more often showed how. He never reduced work to drudgery, but rather elevated it to excitement. Instead of concentrating power, he generated co-operation. He never drove His disciples forward, but was always out in front, leading them to green pastures and oases of still waters.

What does the couplet mean: "As we are, God once was. As God is, we may become?" (Atrr. to Lorenzo Snow).

Alma spoke of a "restoration (that) shall come to all, both old and young, both bond and free, both male and female, both the wicked and the righteous; and even there shall not so much as a hair of their heads be lost; but every thing shall be restored to its perfect frame." (Alma 11:44). Although "it doth not yet appear what we shall be, (nevertheless) we know that, when he shall appear, we shall be like him, for we shall see him as he is." (1 John 3:2). Our hope of a glorious resurrection hinges upon this truth, however dimly it may now be perceived.

In the game of life, how is the Gospel our personal play-book?

The beauty of the Gospel is that one size fits all. It is designed to meet the needs of all of Heavenly Father's children. It is universally applicable, allowing each of us to break free from our limiting beliefs, those stories we tell ourselves that cause us to sabotage our own best efforts. In every case, its doctrines unleash the power of our potential. It is full of magical principles patiently waiting for our wits to grow sharper, that they might inspire us.

126.

> We are baptized because this life is
> the time for us to prepare to
> meet our Heavenly Father.
> (See Alma 32:34).

How can we allow baptism to heal our wounds?

We cannot climb to the summit of Mount Zion while carrying the heavy burden of sin. Who shall ascend into the hill of the Lord," asked the Psalmist, "or who shall stand in his holy place? He that hath clean hands, and a pure heart, who hath not lifted up his soul unto vanity, nor sworn deceitfully." (Psalms 24:3-4).

How can we safeguard our free will, as we prepare for our heavenly homecoming?

Because of our baptism, we are at risk of the unrelenting assaults of Satan upon our spiritual identities. We realize that only God can sustain our spiritual health, by maintaining the stability and integrity of our moral shields. We acknowledge the power of His priesthood as a key element in our fight against Satan's onslaughts. We recognize the inadequacy of own puny efforts, and trust the Savior to come to our rescue, and in particular, to heal the damage done in consequence of the weaknesses in our own armor.

How can baptism help us to exercise agency to act independently?

Baptism impels us to be true to our friends, family, and acquaintances, and to our word. We honor our commitments, in order to draw upon the power of God through ordinances and covenants. We are absolutely honest in our dealings with our fellow warriors, and right the wrongs for which we are responsible. We constantly monitor our defensive network of systems designed to resist Satan, recognize when they fail, accept responsibility for the negative outcomes that are a consequence of our shortcomings, and take steps to restore the integrity of our shield wall of faith by drawing upon the power of the Atonement.

How can the Atonement prepare us to meet God?

We do everything within our ability to maintain open lines of communication with the powers of heaven. We not only believe in Christ, but also believe Him when He says that He can heal us through His Atonement. We then rely upon the Atonement as our secret weapon in the defense of our spiritual identity.

We are baptized to guard ourselves against spiritual identity theft.

How bold is Satan in his efforts to steal our spiritual identity?

He is so brash that he even tried to steal the Savior's identity on the Mount of Temptations. He brazenly demanded that Jesus renounce His citizenship in heaven in exchange for pride, the honors of men, and the admiration of the world. "If thou be the Son of God," he cried, "command that these stones be made bread." (Matthew 4:3). "If thou be the Son of God," he urged, "cast thyself down." (Matthew 4:6). "All these things will I give thee," he promised, "if thou wilt fall down and worship me." (Matthew 4:10).

Do the scriptures reassure us that we are the children of God?

On one occasion, Heavenly Father spoke to Joseph Smith and said: "Thou art Joseph." (D&C 3:9). He likewise told a great Book of Mormon prophet: "Thou art Nephi." (Helaman 10:6), and He told Moses: "Thou art my son." (Moses 1:4). On another occasion, He explained: "Thou art one in me, a son of God; and thus may all become my sons." (Moses 6:68). Thus, was Moses inspired to exclaim: "Thou hast said, I know thee by name." (Exodus 33:12).

How can we be protected against spiritual identity theft?

Baptism helps us to discern good from evil, because Satan wears many hats. He is an honorary member of the Screen Actor's Guild, and a much sought-after image consultant. He methodically cruises the Internet, and is a permanent resident of chat-rooms. He is the great deceiver who bombards us with spam emails. He is a prize-winning author, a talented composer, a lyricist, and a scriptwriter. He is the creative influence behind media too numerous to mention. He is a fashion designer, travel agent, vintner and beer distributor, an actor, newscaster, politician, scientist and power broker. He may even be a teacher, or wear the vestments of the clergy.

How does baptism reinforce the concept that we are children of God?

The scriptures testify that we have a Father in Heaven. Of this truth, there is no doubt, for "the Spirit itself beareth witness with our spirit, that we are the children of God." (Romans 8:16). We know this intuitively. How sweet it is to hear Primary age children as young as three sing the songs of Zion that reinforce what the Spirit whispers to each of us, that we are the children of God.

We are baptized as a testament that "the works,
and the designs, and the purposes of
God cannot be frustrated, neither
can they come to naught."
(D&C 3:1).

What is The Merciful Plan of The Great Creator? (2 Nephi 9:6).

"Mercy claimeth the penitent, and mercy cometh because of the atonement; and the atonement bringeth to pass the resurrection of the dead; and the resurrection of the dead bringeth back men into the presence of God. For behold, justice exerciseth all his demands, and also mercy claimeth all which is her own; and thus, none but the truly penitent are saved." (Alma 42:23-24). Our desire to be baptized is ignited by a celestial spark that God has put into each of His children, in order to save their souls.

What is The Plan of Our God? (2 Nephi 9:13).

The covenant of baptism was "prepared from the foundation of the world." (Alma 42:26). John Taylor taught: "To the Son is given the power of the resurrection, the power of the redemption, the power of salvation, the power to enact laws for the carrying out and accomplishment of the design. Hence, life and immortality are brought to light, the Gospel is introduced, and He becomes the Author of eternal life and exaltation."

What is The Great and Eternal Plan of Deliverance From Death? (2 Nephi 11:5).

One of the foundation teachings of the Gospel is that we came into this world to die. "And now behold, I say unto you that if it had been possible for Adam to have partaken of the fruit of the tree of life at that time, there would have been no death, and the word would have been void." (Alma 12:23). It was clearly understood before we came to earth that our experience here would end with the death of our mortal bodies as part of the Merciful Plan of our Father. When Adam and Eve were placed in the Eden, it was with the understanding that they would transgress God's law and become mortal. (See Moses 6:64). It was no coincidence that shortly after their expulsion from the Garden, clothed in the habiliments of mortality, they were baptized. (See Moses 6:64).

What is The Plan of Salvation? (Alma 24:14).

The Plan of Salvation makes possible the resurrection of otherwise imperfect beings to eternal lives of glory. If it had not been for The Plan, "which was laid from the foundation of the world, there could have been no resurrection of the dead." (Alma 12:25).

We are baptized as a testament that we are willing to participate in "God's eternal plan."
(Official Declaration 2).

What is The Plan of Redemption? (Alma 29:2).

"According to Justice, The Plan of Redemption could not be brought about," and "mercy could not take effect except it should destroy the work of Justice." (Alma 42:13). The beauty of the perfect Plan of Redemption, then, is that it meets the demands of Justice through the infinite mercy of our loving Heavenly Father. With elegant reconciliation, the Plan allows Him to be both just and merciful at the same time. Cherubim and a flaming sword guarded the way to the Tree of Life, providing Adam and Eve with a way, through the Atonement, to fulfil the measure of their creation. (See D&C 88:19).

What is The Great Plan of The Eternal God? (Alma 34:9).

If we take The Great Plan of the Eternal God for granted, or if we abandon its core principles, its power to bless our lives may slip away and be lost forever. The Plans' guarantee of free will gives us wide latitude to inappropriately use our agency to make poor choices. But it also provides us with the currency of faith, that the Atonement might use that legal tender to ransom our souls from spiritual death.

What is The Great and Eternal Plan of Redemption? (Alma 34:16).

The principles governing the Fall of Adam and the Atonement of Jesus Christ, are "great and eternal purposes (that) were prepared from the foundation of the world." (Alma 42:26).

What is The Great Plan of Redemption? (Alma 34:31).

The Plan of Redemption required that "an atonement should be made; therefore God Himself atoneth for the sins of the world, to bring about The Plan of Mercy, to appease the demands of Justice, that God might be a perfect, just God, and a merciful God also." (Alma 42:15). The Atonement allowed Heavenly Father to become the Master of the situation by placating Justice while still mercifully reclaiming us from physical and spiritual death. With the sacrifice of our Savior and all power given to Him, the debt would be paid, redemption made, the covenant fulfilled, Justice satisfied, and the will of God the Father done.

> We are baptized we might lend support
> to the declaration of the Gods
> "that their plan was good."
> (Abraham 4:21).

What is The Plan of Restoration? (Alma 41:2).

The purpose of the Fall was to give us the opportunity to come to the earth in order to prepare for our resurrection. (See Alma 12:24). Through the Atonement and by the grace of God, when we are raised in the resurrection, we will be clothed in exactly the kinds of bodies needed to dwell in the various degrees of glory to which we have qualified, and within which we will feel comfortable.

What is The Great Plan of Salvation? (Alma 42:5).

Without baptism, we are doomed to suffer in the shadows and experience only illusions of reality. Without baptism, sooner or later the discrepancy between our marginalized behavior and the ideals of The Plan will become so great that our short-lived pleasure in worldly ways must evaporate as the morning dew in the light of day. When this disparity reaches "critical mass," the requisite readjustment will tear down the façade of our corruption and hypocrisy to allow the cultivation of a more nurturing lifestyle only made possible by obedience to the principles of the Plan.

What is The Great Plan of Happiness? (Alma 42:8).

Without repentance we must ultimately be in a wretched state, living forever in our sins. (See Alma 12:26). Without baptism, if we were to partake of the fruit of the tree of life, which is eternal life or the highest expression of the love of God, it would not be possible to sustain a celestial existence, inasmuch as in that condition we would be incapable of obedience to celestial principles. Thus, The Great Plan of Happiness would be frustrated. Mercy and Justice were placed before Adam, to bar the way to the Tree of Life until he had the opportunity to participate in the saving ordinances of the Gospel. (See Alma 12:21, 42:2, and Moses 4:31).

What is The Plan of Mercy? (Alma 42:15).

The Plan of Mercy honors the principle of agency, allowing us to encounter opposition in a mortal setting and gain experience. It takes into account the fact that Justice must be served should we violate eternal law in the process. When the Lamb of God was slain from the foundation of the world, The Plan swung into action, allowing us to die without jeopardizing our eternal destiny. (See Alma 42:6).

131.

> We are baptized with the assurance of "eternal life, which God, that cannot lie, promised before the world began." (Titus 1:2).

What is The Plan of Happiness? (Alma 42:16).

Cherubim insured The Plan of Salvation would not be frustrated. For "if Adam had put forth his hand immediately, and partaken of the tree of life, he would have lived forever, according to the word of God, having no space for repentance." (Alma 42:5). Because of his transgression, Justice demanded that "man became lost forever, yea, they became fallen man. And now, ye see by this that our first parents were cut off both temporally and spiritually from the presence of the Lord." So it was, that "they became subject to follow after their own will," to know the good from the evil, and to have joy therein. (Alma 42:6-7).

What is The Great Plan of Mercy? (Alma 42:31).

If we fail to live up to the laws of the Gospel, The Great Plan of Mercy will intervene in our behalf. If we Recognize our mistakes, experience Remorse for having made them, attempt to make Restitution if our behavior has wronged others, learn from the error and Reform our ways, and Resolve to Refrain from Repeating it, we will be free to continue the path of progress, with a complete Resolution because of the Atonement of our Redeemer, of what would have otherwise been incapacitating short-comings.

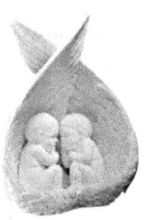

What do the scriptures teach about our pre-mortal life?

The Lord told Jeremiah: "Before I formed thee in the belly I knew thee; and before thou camest forth out of the womb, I sanctified thee, and I ordained thee a prophet unto the nations." (Jeremiah 1:5). Job likewise described a time before we were born, "when the sons of God came to present themselves before the Lord." (Job 1:6).

Do you think that you came to your family here on earth by divine design?

Paul explained that we were chosen "before the foundation of the world, that we should be holy and without blame before him in love. (Ephesians 1:4). "The Preacher, the son of David, king in Jerusalem" (Ecclesiastes 1:1) wrote: "Then shall the dust return to the earth as it was: and the spirit shall return unto God who gave it." (Ecclesiastes 12:7, see also Isaiah 14:12-15, John 3:13, Jude 1:6, Titus 1:1-2, and Revelation 12:2-9).

132.

> We are baptized that, with the gentle instruction of the Spirit, we might become better at building relationships.

Why is it important that we "press forward with a steadfastness in Christ, having a perfect brightness of hope, and a love of God and of all men?" (2 Nephi 31:20).

President David O. McKay once said: "Let me assure you that some day you will have a personal Priesthood interview with the Savior, Himself. If you are interested, I will tell you the order in which He will ask you to account for your earthly responsibilities."

What do you think President McKay said would be the Savior's very first question?

"First, He will request an accountability report about your relationship with your wife."

Since families are the basic building block of eternity, can you imagine what was second on the list of questions?

"Second, He will...request information about your relationship to each and every child."

Since we have all come from God, Who is our Home, what do you think was next on the list?

"Third, he will want to know what you have personally done with the talents you were given in your pre-mortal existence."

133.

We are baptized that we might bow our knees "unto the Father of our Lord Jesus Christ, of whom the whole family in heaven and earth is named." (Ephesians 3:14-15).

Is participation in the programs of the Church important to the Savior?

President McKay said that in our personal interview with the Savior, "He will want a summary of our activity in our Church assignments."

Do you think the Savior will be interested in how we have treated our neighbors?

Since we are all one community, the next thing the Savior will ask, according to President McKay, is: "Were you honest in all your dealings?"

How can we help fulfil the prophecy that the earth shall be "full of the knowledge of the Lord, as the waters cover the sea?" (Isaiah 11:9).

Finally, President McKay said the Savior "will ask for an accountability report on what we have done to contribute in a positive manner to our community, state, country and the world."

How does baptism prepare us for our heavenly reunion with our Father?

"Now are we the sons of God, and it doth not yet appear what we shall be: but we know that, when he shall appear, we shall be like him, for we shall see him as he is." (1 John 3:2).

We are baptized that those who have died without having had the opportunity to hear about The Plan of Salvation might also partake of eternal life.

What does a "patron" do, in the House of The Lord?

The Atonement set the standard for vicarious work. In our day, the Savior has delegated authority to the members of His Church to act vicariously for the dead, who are unable to perform the saving ordinances for themselves, since they have passed beyond the veil and are living in the spirit world while they await the resurrection.

What is vicarious work? (See D&C 138:33).

The ordinances performed by patrons in the temple, beginning with baptism on behalf of those who have passed away, are vicarious works that establish a covenant relationship with our Father. Vicarious work is a key element of The Plan of Salvation, for the Atonement of Jesus Christ itself is such a work.

How does Section 2 of the Doctrine & Covenants relate to baptism for the dead?

Details concerning the coming of Elijah constitute the first revelation Joseph Smith received. It is one of the most carefully documented prophecies of all time, appearing in all four of the Standard Works. (Malachi 4:5-6, 3 Nephi 24 & 25, J.S.H. 1:36-39, and D&C 2 & 110). In fact: "It is the keystone of the wonderful Gospel arch, and if that center stone should weaken and fall out, the whole Gospel structure would topple down in unorganized doctrinal blocks." (John Widtsoe).

Why do you think the wording of Malachi's prophecy is not identical in all four of the Standard Works?

The wording in Malachi in the Bible is identical to 3 Nephi 25:5-6 in The Book of Mormon, but differs from that in the Doctrine and Covenants and the Pearl of Great Price, which are also identical. When Moroni quoted the prophecy to Joseph Smith, his alterations from the Bible and Book of Mormon texts were probably for emphasis and clarification, rather than for correction. The wording helps Latter-day Saints to better understand the prophecy.

135.

> We are baptized as a witness that "the Lord God will do nothing, but he revealeth his secret unto his servants the prophets." (Amos 3:7).

How does Section Two in The Doctrine & Covenants read?

Section 2 reads: "Behold, I will reveal unto you the Priesthood, by the hand of Elijah the prophet, before the coming of the great and dreadful day of the Lord. And he shall plant in the hearts of the children the promises" or covenants "made to the fathers," that is to say, Abraham, Isaac, and Jacob, "and the hearts of the children shall turn" or bind or seal "to their fathers. If it were not so," if the sealing power of the priesthood were not restored, "the whole earth would be utterly wasted at his coming" because The Plan of Salvation would be frustrated. (This is the curse mentioned in Malachi 4:6; see below).

How does the prophecy read in The Old Testament?

Malachi wrote: "Behold, I will send you Elijah the prophet before the coming of the great and dreadful day of the Lord: And he shall turn the heart of the fathers to the children, and the heart of the children to their fathers, lest I come and smite the earth with a curse." (Malachi 4:5-6).

How does the prophecy read in The Pearl of Great Price?

"Behold, I will reveal unto you the Priesthood by the hand of Elijah the prophet, before the coming of the great and dreadful day of the Lord. ...And he shall plant in the hearts of the children the promises" or covenants "made to the fathers," that is to say, Abraham, Isaac, and Jacob, "and the hearts of the children shall turn" or bind or seal "to their fathers. If it were not so," if the sealing power of the priesthood were not restored, "the whole earth would be utterly wasted at his coming." (J.S.H. 1:38-39).

How does the prophecy read in The Book of Mormon?

The Lord quoted Malachi during His ministry among the Nephites: "Behold, I will send you Elijah the prophet before the coming of the great and dreadful day of the Lord; And he shall turn the heart of the fathers to the children, and the heart of the children to their fathers, lest I come and smite the earth with a curse." (3 Nephi 25:6).

> We are baptized that we might be
> "easy to be entreated (and) firm
> to keep the commandments."
> (Helaman 7:7).

How can scriptural aphorisms help us to be easily entreated?

Aphorisms are proverbial statements or theological profundities. They are similar to hokmahs, which are peculiar Hebrew figures of speech. They are sprinkled throughout the liturgy of the Church, testifying to the accuracy of Joseph Smith's translation of ancient Hebraic texts.

How can we use aphorisms to be "firm to keep the commandments?"

All one needs is combustible fuel, an ignition temperature, and oxygen to initiate the conflagration of sin. We must live in the world, but we don't have to be of the world. (See John 15:19). We can't allow the heat of the moment get the better of us. The strait and narrow way has been designed to guide us safely past the ammunition dumps of the devil.

How can aphorisms help us to remember our covenants?

The intoxicating alcohol of the adversary has been distilled to dull our senses, if we are so careless as to indulge in the designer drinks of depravity, debauchery, and decadence. If we are not careful, the hobnailed boots of indiscretion's marathon dancer will tap a rowdy two-step across the terracotta of our consciousness. If we allow excess to be our master, reason will surely be cast into the rumble seat of our libidinous juggernaut. Then, the piper must be paid! (See Pogo, The Cartoon Philosopher).

How can we use our own aphorisms to help us to walk the strait and narrow?

If we do not travel the strait and narrow way, we risk being detoured by doctrinal dilemmas, conceptual cul-de-sacs, and religious roundabout, leading to faltering faith, personality precipices, crises of confidence, accelerating apostasy, and character crippling compromises.

137.

> We are baptized that
> we might be "slow to be led to
> do iniquity; and quick to hearken
> unto the words of the Lord."
> (Helaman 7:7).

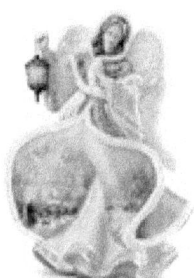

How does our baptism help us to be slow to be led to do iniquity?

Because there needs to be opposition in all things, even the righteous may be seduced by a corrosive cocktail of compromise, spiked by convenience, and offered by a bartender named Beelzebub. This designer drink of the devil may seem palatable, but it is a poisonous potion whose naturally bitter taste of intemperance is only attenuated by all of his counterfeits for joy, such as pleasure, decadence, indulgence, hedonism, and self-gratification.

How are we protected when we are quick to hearken unto the words of the Lord?

If there were a Gospel firearms safety course, it would caution us to avoid chambering rounds of skepticism, incredulity, uncertainty, and criticism in the assault rifle of the adversary. Satan stands like a sentinel who is always anxious to discharge his weapons in the direction of doctrine. Beelzebub's bullets of unbelief may harmlessly ricochet off the bedrock of well-grounded faith. However, his armor-piercing rounds can mortally wound our eternal identity if we do not maintain our moral defensive shields according to the instructions given in the user manual.

Can those who play poker with the devil hope to win every hand?

Those who equivocate walk the slippery slope above a personality precipice, while proper prior priesthood preparation prevents poor performance. In any event, those who are distracted by carnal creations must ultimate crash and burn in the perfect storm of a train wreck in slow motion that has been choreographed by habitually poor choices.

How can aphorisms help us to remember our baptismal covenant?

The scriptures are full of aphorisms, many of which have made their way into the lexicon of the Saints: Ask and you shall receive. Take up your cross, and follow me. There must needs be opposition in all things. Come unto Christ and be perfected in him. Be ye therefore perfect. Keep the commandments. Repent, and be baptized. Charity never faileth. Mercy satisfieth justice. Endure to the end. My yoke is easy, and my burden is light. Come follow me. Faith without works is dead, being alone.

Finally, as Ignatius Loyola declared, we are baptized that we might give and not count the cost, fight and not heed the wounds, toil and not seek for rest, and labor and not ask for any reward save that of knowing that we do God's will.

That we might give and not count the cost...

That we might fight, and not heed the wounds...

That we might toil, and not seek for rest...

That we might labor, and not ask for any reward save that of knowing that we do God's will.

Appendices 1 – 9

One Hundred and One Reasons Why We Are Baptized

1. We are baptized in submission to the law of heaven.

2. We are baptized as a witness that we are willing to follow in the footsteps of the Savior.

3. We are baptized to demonstrate our obedience to the will of the Savior.

4. We are baptized in similitude of the supreme act of humility by the Savior.

5. We are baptized to "fulfill all righteousness." (Matthew 3:15).

6. We are baptized to receive a remission of our sins, if we have reached the age of accountability.

7. We are baptized to gain admission to the Lord's church, which is "the only true and living church upon the face of the whole earth" with which He is pleased. (D&C 1:31).

8. We are baptized that we might experience sanctification through fire and the Holy Ghost. (See Mosiah 5:7).

9. We are baptized that we might be spiritually begotten of Christ. (See Mosiah 5:7).

10. We are baptized that our hearts might be changed through faith on the name of Jesus Christ. (See Mosiah 5:7).

11. We are baptized that we might be born of Jesus Christ. (See Mosiah 5:7).

12. We are baptized in a symbolic re-birth, as we pass through a tangible portal in the similitude of the grave.

13. We are baptized in order to qualify for the blessings that are found in the other ordinances of the Gospel.

14. We are baptized that we might be better prepared to travel the established path that leads to the Celestial Kingdom of God.

15. We are baptized in the temporal expression of a spiritual reality.

16. We are baptized that we might overcome spiritual death, and come into the presence of the Father, the Son, and the Holy Ghost.

17. We are baptized in a palpable expression of the Doctrine of Christ.

18. We are baptized to facilitate the temporal implementation of The Plan of Salvation. (See D&C 3:1).

19. We are baptized that we might have opportunities to bear each other's burdens. (See Mosiah 18:8).

20. We are baptized that we might be given the privilege to "mourn with those that mourn." (Mosiah 18:9).

21. We are baptized that we might "comfort those that stand in need of comfort." (Mosiah 18:9).

22. We are baptized that we might have the courage to "stand as witnesses of God at all times and in all things, and in all places that (we) may be in." (Mosiah 18:9).

23. We are baptized that we might "be redeemed of God, and be numbered with those of the first resurrection, that (we might) have eternal life." (Mosiah 18:9).

24. We are baptized as a witness that we have made a covenant to serve God "and keep his commandments, that he (might) pour out his Spirit more abundantly" upon us. (Mosiah 18:10).

25. We are baptized that we might be given the tools we need to lengthen our stride.

26. We are baptized that we might no more be "strangers and foreigners," but instead, "fellow citizens with the saints, and of the household of God." (Ephesians 2:19).

27. We are baptized that we might join the ranks of member missionaries.

28. We are baptized that we might continue "steadfastly in the apostles' doctrine and fellowship, and in breaking of bread, and in prayers." (Acts 2:41-42).

29. We are baptized that we might be clothed with spiritual chain-mail, as protection against the fiery darts of the adversary. (See 1 Nephi 15:24).

30. We are baptized that we might be released from bondage to sin. (See D&C 84:49).

31. We are baptized that we might participate in the foundation ordinance of The Plan of Salvation.

32. We are baptized by immersion in water, that we might feel not only the spiritual significance, but also the physical intensity, of the covenant we make with our Heavenly Father.

33. We are baptized as Jesus Christ invites us, by name, to become His disciples.

34. We are baptized in a dramatic validation of the influence of the Light of Christ, and of the power of the Holy Ghost.

35. We are baptized to affirm the innocence of little children.

36. We are baptized that we might experience spiritual delight, without the rush of sensory over stimulation that is prevalent in our technological world.

37. We are baptized "for the perfecting of the saints, for the work of the ministry, (and) for the edifying of the body of Christ." (Ephesians 4:12).

38. We are baptized that we might "all come in the unity of the faith, and of knowledge of the Son of God...unto the measure of the stature of the fulness of Christ." (Ephesians 4:13).

39. We are baptized "that we henceforth be no more children, tossed to and fro." (Ephesians 4:14).

40. We are baptized that we might speak "the truth in love, (and) grow up into him in all things, which is the head, even Christ." (Ephesians 4:15).

41. We are baptized "unto the confounding of false doctrines and laying down of contentions." (2 Nephi 3:12).

42. We are baptized that the light of our lives might grow "brighter and brighter until the perfect day." (D&C 50:24).

43. We are baptized that the earth might "be full of the knowledge of the Lord, as the waters cover the sea." (Isaiah 11:9).

44. We are baptized to capture the promise of the "peace of God, which passeth all understanding." (Philippians 4:7).

45. We are baptized that we might pause, and reflect upon the things that are really important in our lives.

46. We are baptized that we might affirm our faith in the immortality of our souls, because we feel, within ourselves, immortal longings.

47. We are baptized that we might learn to abide by the laws of the Celestial Kingdom, even as we dwell upon the earth, that our hearts might burn within us, as the Spirit speaks to us and opens the scriptures to our understanding. (See Luke 24:32).

48. We are baptized that we might think less about self-sufficiency, and more about our Christ dependency.

49. We are baptized that we might be given the tools to burst free of our self-imposed limitations.

50. We are baptized "in consequence of the evils and designs which do and will exist in the hearts of conspiring men (and women) in the last days." (D&C 89:4).

51. We are baptized that we might publish peace and tidings of great joy, endure to the end, and be lifted up at the last day, to inherit eternal life. (See 1 Nephi 13:37).

52. We are baptized that we might enjoy the Sabbath day, as we never have before.

53. We are baptized that we might re-connect with our spiritual Birth Parents.

54. We are baptized that we might enter into God's Rest.

55. We are baptized that we might vitalize Heavenly Father's Plan of Happiness in our lives.

56. We are baptized that we might forever thereafter commemorate the birthdate of our immortal souls.

57. We are baptized that we might have hope in our Savior, Jesus Christ.

58. We are baptized in a process of generation, and not just of maturation. (See Mosiah 27:26).

59. We are baptized that we might enter into the fold, there to be cared for by the Good Shepherd. (See John 10:11).

60. We are baptized that we might contribute our own chapter to The Greatest Story Ever Told.

61. We are baptized that our Heavenly Father might create, in our behalf, an impenetrable "shield of faith" in our Lord Jesus Christ. (Ephesians 6:16).

62. We are baptized in white clothing, to symbolically express the purity of the ordinance and the proximity of the Spirit.

63. We are baptized that the Spirit of the Lord Omnipotent might work "a mighty change in us, or in our hearts, that we have no more disposition to do evil, but to do good continually." (Mosiah 5:2).

64. We are baptized "through the infinite goodness of God, (that by) the manifestations of his Spirit (we might) have great views of that which is to come." (Mosiah 5:3).

65. We are baptized that we might evenly distribute the weight of our temporal baggage, that we might more easily "enter in at the strait gate." (Matthew 7:13).

66. We are baptized that the "opposition in all things" to which Lehi alluded, might become a blessing that allows us to more fully engage The Plan of Salvation. (2 Nephi 2:11).

67. We are baptized that our trials and tribulations might give us experience, and work to our benefit. (See D&C 122:7).

68. We are baptized that the "redemption exemption" that is a codicil to the Law of Justice might be activated and the Law of Mercy set in motion, as our lease on life is renegotiated in our favor.

69. We are baptized that we might make a simple public statement about a profound private conviction.

70. We are baptized "that we might speak with the tongue of angels, and shout praises unto the Holy One of Israel." (2 Nephi 31:13).

71. We are baptized that our hearts might be "knit together in unity and in love." (Mosiah 18:21).

72. We are baptized that we might enjoy the companionship of "the Comforter, which showeth all things, and teacheth the peaceable things of the kingdom." (D&C 39:6).

73. We are "baptized as a witness and a testimony that (we are) willing to serve God with all (our) hearts." (Mosiah 21:35).

74. We are baptized in such a manner that, as we step out of the font, our faces will always be oriented toward the light.

75. We are baptized that we might pursue the object and design of our existence, which is to be the happiest people upon the face of the earth.

76. We are baptized because, as disciples of Christ, it is our lot in life to be sent forth as sheep in the midst of wolves. (See Matthew 10:16).

77. We are baptized that we might receive the means to calibrate our lives with the pattern of heaven itself.

78. We are baptized that the Lord might be on our right, and on our left, and in our hearts. (See D&C 84:88).

79. We are baptized that we might more easily memorize our lines in Heavenly Father's Three Act Play that is entitled "The Plan of Salvation."

80. We are baptized that we might become as lights that are set on a hill. (See Matthew 5:14).

81. We are baptized that our vessels might be filled with the "oil of gladness". (See Hebrews 1:9 & Matthew 25:1).

82. We are baptized to wash away the cobwebs from our minds.

83. We are baptized that the anchors of our faith might rest within a foundation of rock, and not of sand. (See Matthew 7:26).

84. We are baptized that we might fan with faith the fire of our resolve. (See Jeremiah 20:9).

85. We are baptized that we might leave a light burning for those who are late to arrive at the wedding feast. (See John Chapter 2).

86. We are baptized that we might learn how to consecrate to the Lord our time, talents, means, and everything else with which He has blessed us.

87. We are baptized that we might accept our Heavenly Father's invitation to join Him in His work and glory, which is to bring about our immortality and eternal life. (See Moses 1:39).

88. We are baptized that we might rejoice in our characteriztion as a peculiar people. (See 1 Peter 2:9).

89. We are baptized that righteousness might stay the sword of justice that hangs over a wicked world. (See Helaman 13:5).

90. We are baptized that others might be influenced to follow our Exemplar. (See John 14:6).

91. We are baptized that our Latter-day Saint culture might help to insulate us from worldly influences.

92. We are baptized that we might not be tempted to "look back," as we flee from Sodom and Gomorrah. (See Genesis 19:16).

93. We are baptized that we might become new creatures in Christ. (See 2 Corinthians 5:17).

94. We are baptized that we might stand tall for those who may lack the power to do so themselves.

95. We are baptized that we might light candles rather than curse the darkness.

96. We are baptized that it might become easier to approach the Lord with our sacrifices.

97. We are baptized that we might be given opportunities to make and keep the covenants of salvation and exaltation.

98. We are baptized that we might unite ourselves with the ordained process by which eternal principles are communicated.

99. We are baptized that, henceforth, we be no more "carried about with every wind of doctrine." (Ephesians 4:14).

100. We are baptized that we might not be deceived "by the sleight of men, and cunning craftiness, whereby they lie in wait to deceive." (Ephesians 4:14).

101. We are baptized that we might honor the order of the priesthood.

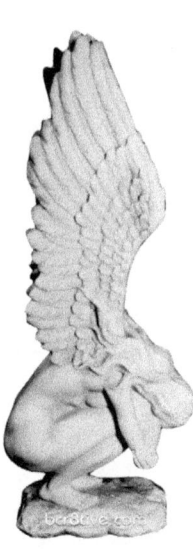

Three Dozen Additional Reasons Why We Are Baptized.

(How many more can you think of?)

102. We are baptized that we might be perfected in our Savior, Jesus Christ. (See Moroni 10:32).

103. We are baptized that, through God's infinite goodness and the manifestations of the Spirit, we might have great views of that which is to come. (See Mosiah 5:3).

104. We are baptized that we might understand how and what we worship, that we might come unto our Father in the name of our Savior Jesus Christ. (See D&C 93:19).

105. We are baptized with the realization that when the Lord gives us commandments, He also prepares ways for us to accomplish the tasks that are set before us. (See 1 Nephi 3:7).

106. We are baptized to make it easier for us to "pray unto the Lord, (to) call upon his holy name, (and to) make known his wonderful works among the people." (D&C 65:4).

107. We are baptized so that, although we were an hungered, and thirsty, and strangers, we will no longer be naked, or sick, or imprisoned within the fortress of our own limiting beliefs. (See Matthew 25:34-40).

108. We are baptized that, with uplifted hands unto the Most High, our incomings, our outgoings, and our salutations might be in the name of the Lord. (See D&C 109:9).

109. We are baptized that we might find greater happiness, peace, and rest; that we might seek for the blessings of the fathers, including the authority to administer the ordinances of the Gospel. (See Abraham 1:2).

110. We are baptized to become more observant followers of righteousness, to possess greater knowledge, to be the progenitors of nations and ambassadors of peace, and to receive instruction, and keep the commandments. (See Abraham 1:2).

111. We are baptized that we might become kings and priests, and queens and priestesses; in effect, to become rightful heirs of the blessings that belonged to the fathers. (See Abraham 1:2).

112. We are baptized because we have brought forth fruit worthy of repentance. (See Moroni 6:1).

113. We are baptized that we might give away all of our sins, but there are strings attached. (See Alma 22:18).

114. We are baptized when charity has become the foundation of our faith.

115. We are baptized beause we have determined to follow the Savior "with full purpose of heart, acting no hypocrisy and no deception before God." (2 Nephi 31:13).

116. We are baptized that we might experience liberation from our self-defeating behaviors.

117. We are baptized that we might press forward with steadfastness, having a perfect brightness of hope and a love of God and of our brothers and sisters, feasting upon the scriptures, and enduring to the end in righteousness. (See Nephi 31:20).

118. We are baptized that we might hear the voice of the Lord that is unto all, for "there is none to escape; and there is no eye that shall not see, neither ear that shall not hear, neither heart that shall not be penetrated." (D&C 1:2).

119. We are baptized that we might affirm our support of family values.

120. We are baptized that we might become saviors on Mount Zion to our kindred dead. (See Obadiah 1:2).

121. We are baptized that the Spirit might find expression as a light within each of us.

122. We are baptized that Heavenly Father might show us our weaknesses. (See Ether 12:27).

123. We are baptized that we might know that we are here, at this place, and in this time, by divine design. (See 2 Nephi 2:24).

124. We are baptized that we might honor God, and feel His love, as we confess His hand in all things, and obey His commandments. (See D&C 59:21).

125. We are baptized to remind ourselves that the poor, the unlearned, the common person, and the native born, may equally come unto Christ. (See Acts 10:24).

126. We are baptized because this life is the time for us to prepare to meet our Heavenly Father. (See Alma 32:34).

127. We are baptized to guard ourselves against spiritual identity theft.

128. We are baptized as a testament that "the works, and the designs, and the purposes of God cannot be frustrated, neither can they come to naught." (D&C 3:1).

129. We are baptized as a testament that we are willing to participate in "God's eternal plan." (Official Declaration 2).

130. We are baptized that we might lend support to the declaration of the Gods "that their plan was good." (Abraham 4:21).

131. We are baptized with the assurance of "eternal life, which God, that cannot lie, promised before the world began." (Titus 1:2).

132. We are baptized that, with the gentle instruction of the Spirit, we might become better at building relationships.

133. We are baptized that we might "bow our knees unto the Father of our Lord Jesus Christ, of whom the whole family in heaven and earth is named." (Ephesians 3:14-15).

134. We are baptized that those who died without having had the opportunity to hear about The Plan of Salvation might also partake of eternal life.

135. We are baptized as a witness that "the Lord God will do nothing, but he revealeth his secret unto his servants the prophets." (Amos 3:7).

136. We are baptized that we might be "easy to be entreated, (and) firm to keep the commandments." (Helaman 7:7).

137. We are baptized that we might be "slow to be led to do iniquity, and quick to hearken unto the words of the Lord." (Helaman 7:7).

138. Finally, as Ignatius Loyola declared, we are baptized that we might give and not count the cost, that we might fight and not heed the wounds, that we might toil and not seek for rest, and that we might labor and not ask for any reward save that of knowing that we do God's will.

Over 500 Discussion Questions

1. We are baptized in submission to the law of heaven.

Do you think baptism has always been performed in the Lord's own way?

How do some people "wrest the scriptures" that relate to baptism? (D&C 10:63).

Do you think the Savior's Apostles administered baptism correctly?

What happened when the priesthood authority of the Apostles died with them?

2. We are baptized as a witness that we are willing to follow in the footsteps of the Savior.

What does it mean to follow the Savior with full purpose of heart? (See Mosiah 7:33).

Why doesn't The Book of Mormon make any special mention of the manner of baptism among the Nephites?

When was the ordinance of baptism first administered?

In the scriptures, where do we learn about Adam's baptism?

3. We are baptized to demonstrate our obedience to the will of the Savior.

How did the voice of the Lord teach Nephi about the ordinance of baptism?

How difficult is it to follow the commandment to be baptized?

What happens when we surrender our will to the guidance of our Heavenly Father?

How can baptism influence our attitude about obedience?

4. We are baptized in similitude of the supreme act of humility by the Savior.

Why do you think the Savior chose to be baptized in the Jordan River?

How can our baptism help us to feel good about ourselves?

How is baptism related to the Atonement of Jesus Christ?

Why do you think the age of eight is described as the age of accountability? (See D&C 29:47).

We are baptized to fulfill all righteousness.
(See Matthew 3:15).

How can envisioning our own baptism make us feel so good inside?

Why do you think the Savior, Who was without sin, submitted to baptism?

How can parents help their children to "fulfill all righteousness" by encouraging them to be baptized? (2 Nephi 31:5).

What else can parents do to prepare their children for baptism?

We are baptized to receive a remission of our sins, if we have reached the age of accountability.

What has the Atonement of Jesus Christ got to do with baptism?

Why do you think God has given us the commandment to be baptized?

Who are the only perfect examples of those who are free from the stain of sin?

What can happen to the innocence of children if they are not baptized at the age of eight?

We are baptized to gain admission to the Lord's church, which is "the only true and living church upon the face of the whole earth" with which He is pleased. (D&C 1:30).

How is baptism Heavenly Father's formal invitation to come into the Savior's fold and to be called His people? (See Mosiah 18:8).

What other qualities must we have, before we are baptized?

How does baptism help to create a Zion society?

To whom is admission to the Lord's Church reserved?

We are baptized that we might experience sanctification through fire and the Holy Ghost. (See Mosiah 5:7).

What is one of the special responsibilities of the Holy Ghost?

How does it make you feel to know that Heavenly Father is a party to every Gospel covenant, including baptism?

Why must we be baptized before we can receive the gift of the Holy Ghost?

What kinds of worldly influences are constantly at work to drive away the Spirit?

9. We are baptized that we might be spiritually begotten of Christ. (See Mosiah 5:7).

What was the experience of Joseph Smith following his own baptism?

What did Jesus teach Nicodemus about being "born again," (John 3:3) and about being "spiritually begotten?" (Mosiah 5:7).

How does The Plan of Salvation make it easier for us to be more sensitive to the whisperings of the Spirit?

How can baptism help us to edit the story of our lives?

10. We are baptized that our hearts might be changed through faith on the name of Jesus Christ. (See Mosiah 5:7).

How is our desire to be baptized linked to faith?

What blessings do we receive as our hearts are changed through faith?

How would you describe your faith in Christ?

How did you develop your faith?

11 We are baptized that we might be born of Jesus Christ. (See Mosiah 5:7).

Why would the prophets teach that it is necessary to be born again? (See Mosiah 5:7).

How can baptism help us to internalize eternal principles? (See Jeremiah 31:33).

For what purpose is the law driven into our inward parts? (See Jeremiah 31:33).

How can baptism heal our spiritual blindness? (See John 9:39-41).

12 We are baptized in a symbolic re-birth, as we pass through a tangible portal in the similitude of the grave.

What is the "similitude of the grave?" (D&C 128:13).

To what end are we re-born?

What did the Savior teach the Nephites about the symbolism of baptism?

What was the instruction given by the Apostle Paul, that related to baptism?

13 We are baptized in order to qualify for the blessings that are found in the other ordinances of the Gospel.

What has the Savior promised to give us when we are baptized?

What blessings may we receive when we are baptized?

How does our baptism qualify us to call ourselves Christians? (See Acts 26:28).

Are the guidelines for baptism subject to private interpretation? (See 2 Peter 1:20).

14 We are baptized that we might be better prepared to travel the established path that leads to the Celestial Kingdom of God.

How does baptism make it easier for us to return to our Heavenly Home?

After our baptism, how does the path that leads back Home open up before us?

How does the Plan hold "the key to the mysteries of the kingdom?" (D&C 84:19).

In what ways is baptism our R.S.V.P. to the invitation that has been sent out across the heavens from our Heavenly Father?

15
We are baptized in the temporal expression of a spiritual reality.

How is baptism a "type?"

How are Gospel principles different from the shifting values of the world?

Why do you think Heavenly Father chose water as the medium to convey spiritual truth?

How is baptism related to our adoption into the House of Israel?

16
We are baptized that we might overcome spiritual death, and come into the presence of the Father, the Son, and the Holy Ghost.

Why do you think the baptismal prayer addresses Heavenly Father, as well as Jesus Christ, and the Holy Ghost?

Why do you think Heavenly Father bore His testimony at the baptism of His Son?

How does the Light of Christ influence us to come to the waters of baptism?

Have you ever wondered how the Holy Ghost completes the "Holy Trinity?"

17. We are baptized in a palpable expression of the Doctrine of Christ.

Where in the scriptures has the Doctrine of Christ been most clearly articulated?
Whose doctrine is it that finds expression in the Gospel?
How does the Holy Ghost help us to recognize the Doctrine of Christ?
How does baptism help us to maintain our focus on the Doctrine of Christ?

18. We are baptized to facilitate the temporal implementation of the Plan of Salvation. (See D&C 3:1).

Have you ever thought about how brilliantly The Plan of Salvation has been scripted, to prepare us to be reunited with our Heavenly Father?
For what purpose was The Plan of Salvation conceived?
How does The Plan of Salvation help us to bridge the gap between mortality and eternity?
How do the 7 "Rs" prepare us to meet our Heavenly Father?

19. We are baptized that we might have opportunities to bear each other's burdens. (See Mosiah 18:8).

How can we help to bear each other's burdens?

How can we give more freely of ourselves?

How can we provide help to those in need of temporal, emotional, or spiritual assistance without enabling them?

What should we do if we feel someone is not deserving of our help?

20. We are baptized that we might be given the privilege to "mourn with those that mourn." (Mosiah 18:9).

How can our covenant of baptism help us to put smiles on the faces of those who mourn?

How can baptism help those who mourn to look at life with new eyes?

How difficult would it be to face life's hardships without the support of the Gospel?

How does knowing that we are the children of God help us to face the adversity that is a part of life?

21

"We are baptized that we might comfort those that stand in need of comfort." (Mosiah 18:9).

Why is "Comforter" an appropriate name for the Holy Ghost?

Why do you think we are asked to provide comfort to the downtrodden?

How does baptism help us to choose the harder right, instead of the easier wrong?

How does baptism empower us to choose wisely?

22

We are baptized that we might have the courage "to stand as witnesses of God at all times and in all things, and in all places that (we) may be in." (Mosiah 18:9).

What is our responsibility to bear witness of the truth?

How seriously must we take our witness of Christ?

How is our witness of Christ quickened, after our baptism?

Is it possible for all of Heavenly Father's children to be witnesses of Christ?

23 We are baptized that we might "be redeemed of God, and be numbered with those of the first resurrection, that (we might) have eternal life." (Mosiah 18:9).

Why do you think that so many people ignorantly worship an "unknown" God?

How does our desire to be baptized stand in contrast to those who have adopted a lifestyle that falls short of obedience to true principles?

After baptism, what takes places within our hearts as we consecrate our lives to the Savior?

Why is the desire for the world's goods so traumatizing?

24 We are baptized as a witness before our Heavenly Father that we have made a covenant to "serve him and keep his commandments, that he may pour out his Spirit more abundantly" upon us. (Mosiah 18:10).

How does baptism encourage us to listen to the spiritual promptings that nudge us in the direction of our dreams?

As we make covenants with God, how are we transformed?

How do the whisperings of the Spirit encourage us to follow the Savior?

What does it mean to be "elect according to the foreknowledge of God?" (1 Peter 1:2).

26. We are baptized that we might be given the tools we need to lengthen our stride.

After baptism, why does lengthening our stride sometimes cause discomfort?

Why would the Savior urge us to go the second mile? (See Matthew 5:41).

How are we fortified as we lengthen our stride?

How does lengthening our stride push us out of our comfort zones?

26. We are baptized that we be no more "strangers and foreigners," but instead, "fellow citizens with the saints, and of the household of God" (Ephesians 2:19).

How can we enjoy the companionship of the Saints?

What concern did Brigham Young express, relating to the temporal welfare of the Saints?

Why is it important to maintain associations with the Saints?

How does fellowship with the Saints positively influence our ability to live in obedience to the principles of the Gospel?

27. We are baptized that we might join the ranks of member missionaries.

Why did Paul say that we need not be embarrassed by the Gospel of Jesus Christ?

Who are the "elect according to the foreknowledge of God?" (1 Peter 1:2).

Who, among all of Heavenly Father's children, are candidates for baptism?

After we are baptized, how can we be good missionaries? (See D&C 13:1).

28. We are baptized that we might continue "steadfastly in the apostles' doctrine and fellowship, and in breaking of bread, and in prayers." (Acts 2:41-42).

What does it mean to be "firm and steadfast in the faith?" (Helaman 15:8).

After our baptism, what qualities must we develop if we are to provide Gospel instruction to others?

Who are "ministering angels?"

After baptism, how are we prompted by the Spirit?

29 We are baptized that we might be clothed with spiritual chain-mail as protection against the fiery darts of the adversary. (See 1 Nephi 15:14).

How can Heavenly Father help us to resist Satan's temptations?

How does immersion in the waters of baptism extinguish the fiery darts of the adversary?

How can keeping our eyes focused on the Savior help us to look past the temptations of the world?

How are free will, opposition, and baptism related?

30 We are baptized that we might be released from bondage to sin.(See D&C 84:49).

What are the key points of King Benjamin's counsel, that explained how to free ourselves from the stain of sin? (See Alma 5:21).

How do you feel about having prophets to whom we can turn for counsel and guidance?

When we are baptized, Whose name do we take upon ourselves?

Without the guidance of our Heavenly Father, how can we hope to effectively deal with opposition in our lives?

31. We are baptized that we might participate in the foundation ordinance of The Plan of Salvation.

What are "days of probation?"

Why has baptism been likened to being reborn? (See John 3:3).

Why is baptism an essential element in the learning laboratory of life?

How can focusing our thoughts on the Savior make our baptismal covenant more meaningful to us?

32. We are baptized by immersion in water, that we might feel not only the spiritual significance, but also the physical intensity, of the covenant we make with our Heavenly Father.

After our baptism, what can we do to reach out and touch the face of God?

How can baptism help us to discover the personal levels of experience with the Savior?

What might we record in our journals about how we felt at our baptisms?

How can we tingle with the consciousness of our kinship with the infinite?

33 We are baptized as Jesus Christ invites us, by name, to become His discipes.

Is it possible that Heavenly Father knows each of us by our name?
How is the covenant of baptism a two-way promise?
What does our Heavenly Father promise, in return?
What does it mean to have His Spirit to be with us?

34 We are baptized in a dramatic validation of the influence of the Light of Christ, and of the power of the Holy Ghost.

What does it feel like, when Heavenly Father inspires us by the "unspeakable gift of the Holy Ghost?" (D&C 121:26).
For how long will the Holy Ghost strive with us?
How does the Light of Christ lead us to the Holy Ghost?
How can the Light of Christ protect us from the influence of the adversary?

35   We are baptized to affirm the innocence of little children.

How can it be, that from the foundation of the world, little children have been saved? (See D&C 137:10).

Why is the practice of infant baptism heretical?

What did Moroni have to say about baptism and accountability?

How did Moroni link accountability to the baptism of little children?

36   We are baptized that we might experience spiritual delight, without the rush of sensory overstimulation that is prevalent in our technological world.

In what ways is baptism an ordinance dating back to an earlier time, when the pace of life was less hectic?

How does baptism invite us to stay in touch with our five physical senses, while enhancing contact with our spiritual sixth sense?

How is baptism the physical confirmation of a spiritual reality?

How do the Light of Christ and the Gift of the Holy Ghost work together to provide unmatched sensory stimulation?

We are baptized "for the perfecting of the saints, for the work of the ministry, (and) for the edifying of the body of Christ." (Ephesians 4:12).

What is the three-fold mission of the Church?

What did Paul mean by the term: "the body of Christ?"

What does it mean to edify the body of Christ?

How can those who have been baptized help to edify the body of Christ?

We are baptized that we might "all come in the unity of the faith, and of the knowledge of the Son of God...unto the measure of the stature of the fulness of Christ." (Ephesians 4:13).

Why is it important for members of the Church to be unified in their faith?

Why is unity in the faith critical to our survival?

How can baptism help us to become perfect in Christ? (See Moroni 10:32).

What happens to us as we mature in the Gospel?

39

We are baptized "that we henceforth be no more children, tossed to and fro" (Ephesians 4:14).

How does our baptism help us to face the adversity in even our well-balanced mortal experiences?

How does our baptism help us to strengthen our relationship with Jesus Christ?

How should we interact with those who are as children because they do not understand the principles of the Gospel?

How can we nurture understanding when our friends express confusion about the doctrine of baptism?

40

We are baptized that we might speak "the truth in love, (and) grow up into him in all things, which is the head, even Christ" (Ephesians 4:15).

How is it easier to "speak the truth in love" after our baptism?

How can baptism help us to "grow up into him in all things?"

Can the Savior be our head, if we are unwilling to submit to baptism?

How does speaking the truth in love cleanse our inner vessel? (See Alma 60:23).

441

We are baptized "unto the confounding of false doctrines and laying down of contentions." (2 Nephi 3:12).

How does baptism prepare us to confound false doctrines?

In what ways are members of the Church prepared to deal with the laying down of contentions?

How can baptism help us to be more patient as we face our adversaries?

Why is baptism as important a principle today as it has ever been in the past?

442

We are baptized that the light of our lives might grow "brighter and brighter until the perfect day." (D&C 50:24).

What is the light of our lives? (See Mosiah 27:29).

When we came to earth from our heavenly home, do you think we were full of light?

How can we protect our light from encroachment by the darkness that is all around us?

How can our baptism help us to be drawn to the light?

43

We are baptized that the earth might "be full of the knowledge of the Lord, as the waters cover the sea." (Isaiah 11:9).

Why is our participation in The Plan of Happiness important?

How can the baptism of just one person make a positive difference in the world?

How does baptism help us to trace our royal lineage, and teach us who we really are?

How can the knowledge of the Lord increase in the earth, when we are true to our baptismal covenant?

44

We are baptized to capture the promise of "the peace of God, which passeth all understanding." (Philippians 4:7).

How can baptism define the pathway to peace?

How can we find peace in the world today?

How does the world's concept of peace differ from that to which baptism invites us?

Without baptism, can we ever truly be at peace?

45

We are baptized that we might pause and reflect upon those things that are really important in our lives.

Whose reflection do we see when we look down into the still waters of baptism?

What kind of change comes over us at our baptism?

How does the world seek change?

Why is the worship of idols of any kind so destructive?

46

We are baptized that we might affirm our faith in the immortality of the soul, because we feel, within ourselves, immortal longings.

How does it change our outlook on life, to know that we are spiritual beings having mortal experiences?

What does it feel like when the veil seems to be very thin?

What is magical about putting our lives in harmony with the principles of The Plan of Salvation?

Why was the commandment to be baptized given, in the first place?

47

We are baptized that we might learn to abide by the laws of the Celestial Kingdom, even as we dwell upon this telestial world. (See D&C 88:22).

What can happen to us if we wait another day to take advantage of repentance?

What happens if we neglect to honor our baptismal covenant to rely upon the Atonement of Christ by continually repenting of our sins?

When the wicked have no intention of repenting, what do you think will happen when "critical mass" is reached?

Do you think angels take notice of our efforts to be obedient to the laws of heaven?

48

We are baptized that we might think less about self-sufficiency, and more in terms of our Christ dependency.

What do you think it means to "come unto Christ?" (Moroni 10:32).

What are some of the divine attributes that we can all work on after our baptisms?

How does baptism prepare us deal with the challenges of life?

How is our baptism an expression of our conviction that the Savior is the sole source of our protection?

49

We are baptized that we might be given the tools to burst free of our self-imposed limitations.

What happens to us when we keep the Savior in our thoughts?

What happens to us when we lose the guidance of the Holy Ghost?

What happens to us when we are attuned to the whisperings of the Spirit?

Why do we use the expression: "The healing waters of baptism?

50

We are baptized in consequence of the "evils and designs which do and will exist in the hearts of conspiring men (and women) in the last days." (D&C 89:4).

How does baptism invite the protection of heaven?

How can our baptism help us to maintain adequate reserves in our spiritual bank accounts?

How can something as simple as baptism protect us against the comprehensive and organized forces of evil?

What is our best defense against evil?

51
We are baptized that we might publish peace and tidings of great joy, endure to the end, and be lifted up at the last day, to inherit eternal life. (See 1 Nephi 13:37).

How does the Gospel bring the world news of great joy and peace?
What happens to us as we publish peace and glad tidings?
Without baptism, can we generate the spiritual horsepower to worship the Savior with fervency?
How can we strengthen our relationship with the Savior, that He might lift us up at the last day unto eternal life?

52
We are baptized that we might enjoy the Sabbath day, as we never have before.

How does baptism help us to obey the Law of The Sabbath?
For what purpose was the Sabbath day created?
How can baptism help the Sabbath day become more special?
How can baptism turn our hearts to the Law of the Sabbath?

§3 We are baptized that we might re-connect with our spiritual Birth Parents.

How does our baptism allow us to experience mortality while maintaining our connection with the eternities?

How does our baptism expand our understanding of our divine heritage?

How does God answer, when we ask: "Father, are you there?"

How is our baptism related to the sealing power of the priesthood?

§4 We are baptized that we might enter into God's Rest.

How is God's Rest harmonious with family exaltation?

How can baptism generate the power to propel us into God's Rest?

What must we do, in order to be able to enter into God's Rest?

After our baptism, how can we reach out and touch the face of God?

55. We are baptized that we might vitalize Heavenly Father's Plan of Happiness in our lives.

How can our baptism help us to internalize the principles that lead to happiness?

How does our baptism provide opportunities to re-adjust our priorities?

Why is the Gospel the foundation of real happiness?

Why do those who disobey the commandments sometimes seem to be happy?

56. We are baptized that we might forever thereafter commemorate the birthdate of our immortal souls.

Why is our baptism a cause for celebration in heaven?

How does the day of our baptism commemorate the birthdate of our immortal soul?

How does our baptism send a message to heaven that all is well on our mission in mortality, and that one day we will be headed back Home?

Do you think that heavenly beings are given permission to attend baptismal services?

57

We are baptized that we might have hope in our Savior, Jesus Christ.

How does our knowledge of The Plan of Salvation expand the scope of our hope in Christ?
Is hope in Christ reserved only for members of The Church of Jesus Christ of Latter-day Saints?
How can baptism make Saints of sinners?
How does baptism reflect our hope in Christ?

58

We are baptized in a process of generation, and not just of maturation. (See Mosiah 27:26).

How is baptism a mile post on our journey toward becoming new creatures in Christ? (See Mosiah 27:26).
What does it mean to make the journey to Christ?
How does baptism bind us to Heavenly Father's perfect Plan of Salvation?
How does baptism illustrate the genius of our Heavenly Fathers' Plan?

59. We are baptized that we might enter into the fold, there to be cared for by the Good Shepherd.

Why is it dangerous to allow ourselves to become complacent about our baptismal covenant?

How is baptism the gift that keeps on giving?

How does baptism re-define itself each time the penitent faithful enter the healing waters?

How does baptism help us to live in accordance with priesthood principles?

60. We are baptized that we might contribute our own chapter to The Greatest Story Ever Told.

What do you think their reaction will be, when others sit down to read your chapter in The Greatest Story Ever Told?

What tools have you been given to help you to richly illustrate your own chapter in The Greatest Story Ever Told?

Have you noticed how your mentors have modified their approach, when teaching you how to write your story?

How does The Plan of Salvation set us free to reach our potential?

61

We are baptized that our Heavenly Father might create, in our behalf, an impenetrable "shield of faith" in the Lord Jesus Christ. (Ephesians 6:16).

Why do you think we are baptized individually, and not in large groups?
Why is it important to keep our shields of faith bright and shiny?
How do our shields of faith encourage accountability?
Why is baptism integral to our shields of faith?

62

We are baptized in white clothing, that we might symbolically express the purity of the ordinance and our proximity to the Spirit.

Why do we wear white clothing at baptismal services?
Are those who administer the ordinance required to wear white clothing during the Sacrament?
Is there an official Church policy or standard that requires the wearing of white clothing at times other than when performing the baptismal ordinance?
How can baptism help us to have clean hands and pure hearts? (See Psalms 24:4).

63

We are baptized that the Spirit of the Lord Omnipotent might work "a mighty change in us, or in our hearts, that we have no more disposition to do evil, but to do good continually." (Mosiah 5:2).

How does knowing that we are the children of God help to work a mighty change in our behavior?

How do we view the world when our nature has been changed through baptism?

Why does faith always precede the miracle?

How does our baptism kindle vital faith?

64

We are baptized "through the infinite goodness of God, (that by) the manifestations of his Spirit (we might) have great views of that which is to come." (Mosiah 5:3).

How is our spiritual education different from worldly learning?

What happens when we allow the Spirit to teach us?

How does baptism have the power to change behavior?

What happens to those who wait upon the Lord? (See Isaiah 40:31).

182

65

We are baptized that we might evenly distribute the weight of our temporal baggage, that we might more easily "enter in at the strait gate." (Matthew 7:13).

How can baptism help us to more comfortably carry our own burdens?
How can temporal baggage get in the way of our spiritual objectives?
How do you think the Lord views our temporal baggage?
In a world that is overwhelmed by temporal baggage, how can baptism help us to avoid being tainted by it?

66

We are baptized that the "opposition in all things" spoken of by Lehi might become a blessing that allows us to more fully engage The Plan of Salvation. (2 Nephi 2:11).

How can our baptism become the foundation for purposeful action?
How can baptism help us to view opposition as a blessing in disguise?
How can we more fully engage the elements of The Plan of Salvation, in order to more effectively deal with opposition?
How does the Savior help us to manage opposition?

67

We are baptized that our trials and tribulations might give us experience, and be for our good. (See D&C 122:7).

Since opposition is necessary for free will to be exercised, how does baptism allow us to reach our potential without suffering damage to the stature of our spirits?

How can our baptism help us to see more clearly from an eternal perspective?

How can our baptism help us to increase our spiritually aerobic maximum pulse rate, as well as the capacity of our lungs to be filled with celestial air?

How can our baptism teach us how to be comfortable in the company of immortal beings?

68

We are baptized that the "redemption exemption" that is a codicil to the Law of Justice might be activated and the Law of Mercy set in motion, that our lease on life might be renegotiated in our favor.

Why do you think Heavenly Father and the Holy Ghost were present at the baptism of Jesus, to witness the validation of His very special lease on life?

Following baptism, how can we take advantage of our own brand new lease on life?

How does Heavenly Father encourage us to enhance, to our benefit, the terms of our lease on life?

How does baptism strengthen our resolve to be true to our divine destiny?

69

We are baptized that we might make a simple public statement about a profound private conviction.

In what ways can our baptism be unassuming and reflective?

How do our faith and testimony carry us beyond the physical ordinance to the spiritual covenant?

How can the simplicity of the ordinance orient us toward the mysteries of the kingdom?

How is it possible that the 25 simple words of the baptismal ordinance can have such profound meaning?

70

We are baptized "that we might speak with the tongue of angels, and shout praises unto the Holy One of Israel." (2 Nephi 31:13).

How do you think baptism prepares us to receive spiritual gifts?

How is baptism like the Rosetta Stone of spiritual experience?

How can baptism unlock the gift of the interpretation of tongues?

How does baptism prepare us to shout praises unto the Holy One of Israel?

71

We are baptized that our hearts might be "knit togther in unity and in love." (Mosiah 18:21).

How can our baptism help us to make sense of the myriad elements of The Plan of Salvation?

How can baptism assure us that when our time comes to pass through the veil, we will leave behind legacies that contribute to the establishment of Zion?

Can eight year old children be as spiritually prepared for baptism as eighty year old adults?

As baptism knits us together, will there be any missing threads in the pattern He has planned?

72

We are baptized that we might enjoy the companionship of "the Comforter, which sheweth all things, and teacheth the peaceable things of the kingdom." (D&C 39:6).

How is baptism like a commencement exercise?

How can baptism help us to conquer our self-defeating behaviors?

What tools have we been given to nurture our understanding of the peaceable things of the kingdom?

Why is faith without works dead, that it cannot save us? (See J.S.T. James 2:14).

73

We are "baptized as a witness and a testimony that (we are) willing to serve God with all (our) hearts." (Mosiah 21:35).

How can the Light of Christ help us to fulfill our baptismal commitment to minister to the needs of others?

How is witnessing for Christ like a spiritually aerobic exercise program?

How can we follow the example of Aaron?

What are the ordinances of salvation and exaltation?

74

We are baptized in such a way that, as we step out of the font, our faces are oriented toward the light.

During baptismal services, how can we invite the Spirit, that we might reach out and touch the face of God?

Why is it important to keep our faces oriented toward the light? (See D&C 88:118).

What can happen to us if we do not steadfastly face the light?

If we allow it to do so, where will our illuminated path lead us?

75

We are baptized that we might pursue the object and design of our existence, which is to be the happiest people upon the face of the earth.

How can we be strengthened, as we continue our journey to Christ after our baptism?

Do you think our feelings of happiness come from secretions in our brains, or from our Heavenly Father, Who, ironically, created dopamine in the first place?

Why do you think that it is in quiet moments that we most clearly hear the voice of the Spirit?

What kind of spiritual nourishment is served at baptismal celebrations?

76

We are baptized because, as disciples of Christ, it is our lot in life to be sent forth as sheep in the midst of wolves. (See Matthew 10:16).

How can our baptism take us in the direction of our dreams?

How can our baptism help us to maintain order in a chaotic world?

How is baptism an expression of the self-restraint that is required by those who would call themselves disciples of Christ?

How can the Light of Christ protect us from the influence of the adversary?

> We are baptized that we might receive the
> means to calibrate our lives with the
> pattern of heaven itself.

How is baptism related to the Infinite Atonement?

How does the Light of Christ work behind the scenes, to help us fill the measure of our creation?

How important is it to have a correct understanding of "the age of accountability" as it relates to baptism?

How does our baptism allow us to experience mortality, and at the same time establish an undeniable connection with the eternities?

> We are baptized that the Lord might be on
> our right, and on our left, and in
> our hearts. (See D&C 84:88).

What mentors have accompanied you during your journey to the waters of baptism?

As you have made the journey to Christ, how have you felt His presence? (See Alma 37:41).

How does the Savior work through others to guide us?

How does Satan attempt to influence us to abandon the Savior as our traveling companion?

79
We are baptized that we might more easily memorize our lines in Heavenly Father's Three Act Play that is entitled "The Plan of Salvation."

What kinds of distractions does Satan employ to disrupt the execution of The Plan?

How does baptism crystalize our understanding of the Fall of Adam and the Atonement of Jesus Christ?

How does baptism orient us toward the mysteries of eternity that are part of the script of Act Three of The Plan of Salvation?

In the distant past, do you think we shouted for joy upon hearing about The Plan of Salvation?

80
We are baptized that we might become as lights that are set on a hill. (See Matthew 5:14).

What does it mean to magnify our callings? (See D&C 84:33).

How does light manifest itself as inspiration and revelation?

How does the light that emanates from Christ speak to us?

Why is it important to always, always, walk in the light?

81

We are baptized that our vessels might be filled with the "oil of gladness." (See Hebrews 1:9 & Matthew 25:1).

What is the currency of faith that accrues with compound interest to those who have entered the waters of baptism?

How can "the Lord…go before you; and the God of Israel be your rearward?" (Isaiah 52:12).

How do the terms of our lease on life compel us to look with gratitude to the Author of Salvation?

How does baptism prevent us from going "down to the vile dust, from whence (we have) sprung, unwept, unhonored, and unsung?"

82

We are bapized to wash away the cobwebs from our minds.

How does The Book of Mormon clear up confusion in the world regarding the need for those with diminished mental capacity to repent and be baptized?

What discoveries await us, as we "walk in the Light of the Lord" following our baptism? (Isaiah 2:5).

What is captivating about the positive behavior changes that follow baptism?

How can The Book of Mormon help us to better understand the basic principles and doctrines of the Gospel of Jesus Christ?

§3

We are baptized that the anchors of our faith might be secured within a foundation of rock, and not of sand. (See Matthew 7:26).

What are the fruits of faith? (See Alma 32:40).

What did the Savior teach the Nephites about baptism?

How can baptism help us to come to "the knowledge of the Son of God?" (Ephesians 4:13).

How does our baptism provide a foundation of stability in a world that seems to lack moral footings?

§4

We are baptized that we might fan with faith the fire of our resolve. (See Jeremiah 20:9).

What does baptism teach us about self-reliance?

In what ways does baptism empower us?

For how long do you think we can maintain the intensity of the feelings that are generated by baptism?

How can our baptism help us to move beyond the mediocrity that too often defines the lifestyle of those who are mired in the values of the every-day world? (See Isaiah 55:9).

We are baptized that we might leave a light burning for those who are late to arrive at the wedding feast. (See John Chapter 2).

Who among us needs a boost, when life's burdens weigh them down and slow their progress along the path that leads to the waters of baptism?

What is the fate of those who refuse the invitation to be baptized?

As children of light, what can we do to strengthen the testimonies of others?

How can you explain the universality of immortal longings that are experienced by so many of Heavenly Father's children?

We are baptized that we might learn how to consecrate to the Lord our time, talents, means, and everything else with which He has blessed us.

What happens to us when our priorities are out of order?

How does our baptism provide us with opportunities to "give place" or study, pray, and commit ourselves to a purposeful plan of action? (See Alma 32:27).

How does baptism prepare us to more thoughtfully budget our time?

How can baptism help us to turn our attention to the weightier matters of the law? (See Matthew 23:23).

87

We are baptized that we might accept our Heavenly Father's invitation to join Him in His work and glory, which is to bring about our immortality and eternal life. (See Moses 1:39).

How is baptism the key to an understanding of the mission statement of our Father in Heaven? (See Moses 1:39).

What do you think Paul meant, when he taught that there is "one Lord, one faith, (and only) one baptism?" (Ephesians 4:5).

Why is the day of our baptism such a happy occasion?

How has Heavenly Father provided for us, so that we might be assured of eternal life following our baptisms?

88

We are baptized that we might rejoice in our characterization as a peculiar people. (See 1 Peter 2:9).

How can our participation in God's Plan refine us, and thereby become a perfecting process? (See Malachi 3:2).

How does it feel to know that we are on the path of progression?

What principles do you think might have been introduced at the Council in Heaven before our world was created? (See D&C 138:55).

Do you think that baptism might have been one of the hot topics that were discussed at the Council in Heaven? (See D&C 138:56, Abraham 4:26, & 5:2).

89

We are baptized that righteousness might stay the sword of justice that hangs over a wicked world. (See Helaman 13:5).

Do you think the angels in heaven are, even now, taking note of our behavior?

Why does amending behavior require a change of heart, as well?

How can our baptism help us to distinguish good from evil?

How can the Light of Christ have the power to lead the children of God to the waters of baptism?

90

We are baptized that others might be influenced to follow our Exemplar. (See John 14:6).

Why is it important to exercise our testimonies as often as possible?

How does our baptism unleash the power of God within us, that our shields of faith might be fortified?

What has our Creator provided for us to make it easier for us to witness in His name?

What are some of the evidences of the spiritual unification of the members of the Church?

91. We are baptized that the culture of the Latter-day Saints might help to insulate us from worldly influences.

How powerful is the wind of doctrine?

How can baptism help us to recognize the divisive influence of the wind of doctrine?

Why is it that those who base their math on the wind of doctrine always wind up with negative sums?

How can our baptismal covenant help us to face the light, so the shadows will always be behind us?

92. We are baptized that we might not be tempted to "look back," as we flee from Sodom and Gomorrah. (See Genesis 19:16).

Is it necessary to have authority to baptize?

How does Satan use cunning craftiness to penetrate our defenses?

Why don't more people understand that one vote plus God constitutes a majority?

How can our sense of temporal security be deceiving?

93

We are baptized that we might become new creatures
in Christ. (See 2 Corinthians 5:17).

How can the scriptures expand our appreciation of the scope of The Plan of Salvation?
How can baptism, and The Plan of Salvation, put us in touch with our spiritual roots?
What does it mean to have been created in both the image and the likeness of God?
How is it to be accomplished, that the dead might accept the Gospel in the Spirit World?

94

We are baptized that we might stand tall for others
who may lack the power to do so themselves.

Does the Light of Christ influence all of Heavenly Father's children?
How might those who do not correctly understand the ordinance of baptism be "in the gall of bitterness?" (Moroni 8:14).
What might be the best way to talk to our friends about how we feel about our baptism?
Why do you think we, as well as the Ephesian Saints, need to hear Paul's instruction relating to unity? (See Ephesians 2:19).

95
We are baptized that we might light candles rather than curse the darkness.

Can one baptism make a difference in the world, or can one baptism make a world of difference?

Can one baptism stem the advancing tide of wickedness?

How can baptism prepare us for the coming millennial day?

How does our baptism place us on a path that follows priesthood direction?

96
We are baptized that it might become easier to approach the Lord with our sacrifices.

What is the difference between a donation and a sacrifice?

How comprehensive must our sacrifice be, before it is acceptable to the Lord?

What is an honest tithe?

How is the payment of tithing a barometer of our spiritual maturity?

97 We are baptized that we might be given opportunities to make and to keep the covenants of salvation and exaltation.

What was King Benjamin's simple counsel regarding how we can be obedient to our baptismal covenant?

How does King Benjamin's counsel empower us to fill the measure of our creation?

How will our witness for Christ define, delineate, and determine our divine destiny?

How do covenants vitalize the work of the ministry?

98 We are baptized that we might unite ourselves with the ordained process by which eternal principles are communicated.

How can others help us to "give birth" to our participation in the work of the ministry?

How can we make sure that our ministry does not offend people?

How can Heavenly Father, Jesus Christ, and the Holy Ghost infuse the universe with light?

Is there any viable alternative to baptism?

99

We are baptized that, henceforth, we be no more "carried about with every wind of doctrine." (Ephesians 4:14).

What are the winds of doctrine?

How does baptism refute the false notion that we can avoid the consequences of sin by procrastinating the day of our repentance? (See Alma 34).

How has the wind of doctrine penetrated nearly every aspect of the lives of those around us?

How can our baptism be a shield and a protection against the power of the destroyer, as long as we have a work left to do on the earth?

100

We are baptized that we might not be deceived "by the sleight of men, and cunning craftiness, whereby they lie in wait to deceive." (Ephesians 4:14).

What is "the sleight of men?"

How is the spirit that is present at a baptismal service the polar opposite of "cunning craftiness?"

How can baptism offer protection from those who "lie in wait to deceive?"

How can baptism help us to recognize the fingerprints of Satan on the idols with which he tempts us?

101 We are baptized that we might honor the order of the priesthood.

By what authority is baptism performed?
What was Oliver Cowdery's witness, regarding the angelic restoration of the authority to baptize?
Who are the sons of Levi that are referred to in Doctrine & Covenants Section 13?
How does baptism create the opportunity for young men to become the sons of Moses and of Aaron?

102 We are baptized that we might be perfected in our Savior, Jesus Christ. (See Moroni 10:32).

How can baptism fortify us with the discipline to go the second mile?
What happens when we turn to the scriptures to learn about the Father of our spirits?
How does it make you feel to know that Heavenly Father knows each of us by our first name?
How can our baptismal covenant help us to become perfect in our repentance? (See Matthew 5:48).

103

We are baptized that, "through the infinite goodness of God, and the manifestations of the Spirit," we might "have great views of that which is to come." (Mosiah 5:3).

How can baptism help us to achieve spiritual symmetry?

How does our baptism entitle us to the further light and knowledge that the Lord has promised us?

What does it mean to have an eternal perspective?

How does Heavenly Father link baptism to the precious gift of testimony?

104

We are baptized that we might understand how and what we worship, that we might come unto our Father in the name of our Savior Jesus Christ. (See D&C 93:19).

How does our baptism grant us access to the mysteries of the kingdom of heaven? (See Matthew 13:11).

How does baptism free us to worship God "according to the dictates of (our) own conscience?" (11th Article of Faith).

How do you think we felt about coming to earth, after The Plan had been fully explained to us in the pre-mortal world?

Following our baptism, how can the ordinances of the temple become the pinnacle of our worship?

165

We are baptized with the realization that when the Lord gives us commandments, He also prepares ways for us to accomplish the tasks that are set before us. (See 1 Nephi 3:7).

How can sacrifice have the power to make us feel so happy?
How can renewing our covenant of baptism help us to lengthen our stride?
Why do you think there is a need for regular repetitive repentance?
How can angels from heaven help us to repent?

166

We are baptized to make it easier for us to "pray unto the Lord, (and to) call upon his holy name, (and to) make known his wonderful works among the people." (D&C 65:4).

What is our greatest joy, when we sacrifice for the kingdom?
With Heavenly Father taking such good care of us, how can we keep our blessings in perspective?
What is one of the best ways to follow the Savior's example of missionary work?
Can there be a greater witness than the Holy Ghost?

107

We are baptized because, although we were an hungered, and thirsty, and strangers, we are no longer naked, or sick, or imprisoned within the fortress of our own limiting beliefs. (See Matthew 25:34-40).

How does baptism help us to break free of our self-imposed limitations?

How can baptism counteract the fading light of limiting beliefs?

How was Naaman the Leper a prisoner of limiting beliefs?

How can our baptism liberate us from intellectual, philosophical, or spiritual captivity?

108

We are baptized that our incomings, our outgoings, and all our salutations may be in the name of the Lord, with uplifted hands unto the Most High. (See D&C 109:9).

How can witnesses help those who are struggling as they make the journey to Christ?

How does the Light of Christ work tirelessly to encourage us to praise God?

How can the Light of Christ prompt us to lift up our hands and praise God?

How is our baptism a re-affirmation of our pre-mortal acceptance of The Plan of Salvation?

We are baptized that we might find greater happiness, peace, and rest; that we might obtain the blessings of the fathers, including the authority to administer the ordinances of the Gospel.
(See Abraham 1:2).

After the close of the Savior's ministry, how successful was the Church in maintaining strict obedience to the Doctrine of Christ?

How did the Reformation pave the way for the Restoration of the Gospel?

What do you think Thomas Jefferson meant, when he used the term: "Primitive Christianity"?

How is baptism related to the Restoration of the Gospel?

We are baptized to become more observant followers of righteousness, to possess greater knowledge, to be the progenitors of nations, ambassadors of peace, and to receive instruction, and keep the commandments.
(See Abraham 1:2).

What do the scriptures have to say about the ability of the Church to sustain true doctrine without continual revelation?

What did early Church historians have to say about apostasy from the truth?

Why did the Pharisees of His day remain silent when Jesus was baptized?

How can the ordinance of baptism help us to be more observant followers of righteousness?

111 We are baptized that we might become kings and queens, and priests and priestesses; in effect, heirs who hold the rights that belonged to the fathers. (See Abraham 1:2).

Why are we baptized individually, and not in large groups?

What is the eternal destiny of those who die without baptism before they reach the age of accountability?

To whom do the blessings of the Abrahamic Covenant apply?

Where does the pathway lead that begins with baptism?

112 We are baptized because we have brought forth fruit worthy of repentance. (See Moroni 6:1).

How does baptism free us from the natural process of entropy, wherein everything that is of a temporal nature gradually declines into disorder?

Why do you think baptism has been described as a "narrow gate?" (2 Nephi 33:9).

Why do faith and repentance precede baptism? (See the 4th Article of Faith).

After our baptism, when we regularly repent, what happens to the recollection of our former sins?

113
We are baptized that we might give away all of our sins, but there are strings attached. (See Alma 22:18).

What happens when we give away our sins?

Why do you think the Sacrament has been provided to those who have been baptized?

Do you think that we could be happy while living in eternity, if we had not beforehand given away our sins?

Can you think of anyone who would be willing to take personal responsibility for our sins?

114
We are baptized when charity has become the foundation of our faith.

How can we protect ourselves with a "shield of faith?"

Our shield of faith notwithstanding, why does it sometimes seem as if we are so alone? (See Mark 1:3).

How can charity strengthen our "shield of faith?"

How do those who have been baptized qualify by worthiness to bear a "shield of faith?"

115

We are baptized as soon as we have determined to follow the Savior "with full purpose of heart, acting no hypocrisy and no deception before God." (2 Nephi 31:13).

How is our discipleship vitalized as we approach the Savior with full purpose of heart?

How can we give birth to our witness of Jesus Christ, that it might be borne "with full purpose of heart?"

Why do you think that people sometimes act with hypocrisy, or "deception before God?"

What has Heavenly Father provided to make sure that we witness for the Savior with full purpose of heart?

116

We are baptized that we might experience liberation from our self-defeating behaviors.

How does baptism prepare us for our magnum opus in the theater of life?

Why do you think the principles of the Gospel are called "the perfect law of liberty?" (See James 1:25).

How does baptism re-introduce us to the program of the Three Act Play that was imprinted upon our souls before we came to earth?

How does baptism brings out the best in us?

We are baptized that we might press forward with steadfastness, having a perfect brightness of hope and a love of God and of our brothers and sisters, feasting upon the scriptures, and enduring to the end in righteousness. (See Nephi 31:20).

Following baptism, how can we personalize the ordinance of the Sacrament, so that in its repetition, it might become a powerful vehicle for our growth?

How did Joseph Smith feast upon the word of God after reading James 1:2-3 in the New Testament?

Why do you think Joseph Smith received the gift of the ministering of angels even before his baptism?

How does our baptism become a commencement exercise?

We are baptized that we might hear the voice of the Lord that is unto all, for "there is none to escape; and there is no eye that shall not see, neither ear that shall not hear, neither heart that shall not be penetrated." (D&C 1:2).

In what literal and figurative ways does the Savior ask us to follow Him?

How can we follow the Savior by listening to the counsel of His prophet?

How can we follow the Savior if there is confusion regarding the correct administration of the ordinance of baptism?

How does the baptismal prayer in The Book of Mormon help us to follow the Savior?

119 We are baptized that we might affirm our support of family values.

Why does it sometimes seem as if the prophets are as lone voices crying in the wilderness? (See Mark 1:3).

How can the words of the prophets fortify us?

How can baptism empower us to act upon the principles contained in The Proclamation on The Family?

How can baptism protect our family memories from tarnishing?

120 We are baptized that we might become saviors on Mount Zion to our kindred dead. (See Obadaiah 1:21).

How does vicarious work for the dead harmonize with the principles of The Plan of Salvation?

How can all of Heavenly Father's children have equal opportunity to become heirs of salvation and eternal life?

How does baptism for the dead stand beside the Atonement as a vicarious work?

How is baptism for the dead the "most gloribus of all subjects belonging to the everlasting gospel?" (D&C 128:17).

121
We are baptized that the Spirit might find expression as a light within ourselves.

What do you think will be the outcome of the battle raging in the hearts of men, on Saturday?

Why is it important for us to maintain our unique personality signatures?

How does baptism help us to regain and retain our spiritual identities?

What can happen to us, if we do not enjoy the protection from spiritual identity theft, that is afforded by baptism?

122
We are baptized that Heavenly Father might show us our weaknesses. (See Ether 12:27).

How can our weakness be transformed into a source of strength?

How does the grace of God help us to deal with our weaknesses and imperfections?

Why would Heavenly Father think to bless us with weaknesses?

How can a quality like weakness possibly promote a principle that is as positive as progression?

123
We are baptized that we might know that we are here, at this place, and in this time, by divine design.

What do you think the Lord meant, when He said: "All these things shall give thee experience, and shall be for thy good?" (D&C 122:7).

How would you describe the choreography of The Plan of Salvation?

How can The Plan of Salvation be infinite in its scope and yet be so personalized that it meets our individual needs?

What are divine accoutrements?

124
We are baptized that we might honor God and feel His love, as we confess His hand in all things, and obey His commandments. (See D&C 59:21).

Have you ever thought to compare your faith to that of those whom Peter taught on the Day of Pentecost? (See Acts 2:37).

How is the Angel Moroni a prototype for those who will one day be enveloped in light?

How can baptism provide the mortar that binds together the foundation principles of the Pillars of Creation?

How can the Holy Ghost help us to honor our baptismal covenant?

125

We are baptized to remind ourselves that the poor, the unlearned, the common person, and the native born, may equally come unto Christ.

Why do our mortal experiences sometimes build us up, while at other times they seem to tear us down?

How does the Gospel exert an equalizing influence?

Have you ever heard the couplet, penned by Lorenzo Snow, that reads: "As man is, God once was. As God is, man may be?"

As we participate in the game of life, in what ways is the Gospel of Jesus Christ like our own personal play-book?

126

We are baptized because this life is the time for us to prepare to meet our Heavenly Father.
(See Alma 32:34).

How can baptism heal our wounds?

How can we safeguard our free will, as we prepare to meet God?

How can baptism help us to exercise agency to act independently?

How can the Atonement prepare us for our heavenly homecoming?

127 We are baptized to guard ourselves against spiritual identity theft.

How bold is Satan in his efforts to steal our spiritual identity?

Do the scriptures reassure us that we are the treasures of heaven?

How can we be protected against spiritual identity theft?

How does baptism reinforce the concept that we are children of God?

128 We are baptized as a testament that "the works, and the designs, and the purposes of God cannot be frustrated, neither can they come to naught." (D&C 3:1).

What is The Merciful Plan of The Great Creator? (2 Nephi 9:6).

What is The Plan of Our God? (2 Nephi 9:13).

What is The Great and Eternal Plan of Deliverance From Death? (2 Nephi 11:5).

What is The Plan of Salvation? (Alma 24:14).

129

We are baptized as a testament that we are willing to participate in "God's eternal plan" (Official Declaration 2).

What is The Plan of Redemption? (Alma 29:2).

What is The Great Plan of The Eternal God? (Alma 34:9).

What is The Great and Eternal Plan of Redemption? (Alma 34:16).

What is The Great Plan of Redemption? (Alma 34:31).

130

We are baptized we might lend support to the declaration of the Gods "that their plan was good" (Abraham 4:21).

What is The Plan of Restoration? (Alma 41:2).

What is The Great Plan of Salvation? (Alma 42:5).

What is The Great Plan of Happiness? (Alma 42:8).

What is The Plan of Mercy? (Alma 42:15).

131

We are baptized with the assurance of "eternal life, which God, that cannot lie, promised before the world began." (Titus 1:2).

What is The Plan of Happiness? (Alma 42:16).

What is The Great Plan of Mercy? (Alma 42:31).

What do the scriptures teach about our pre-mortal life?

Do you think that you came to your family here on earth by divine design?

132

We are baptized that, with the gentle instruction of the Spirit, we might become better at building relationships.

Why is it important that we "press forward with a steadfastness in Christ, having a perfect brightness of hope, and a love of God and of all men?" (2 Nephi 31:20).

What do you think President McKay said would be the Savior's very first question?

Since families are the basic building block of eternity, can you imagine what was second on the list of questions?

Since we have all come from God, Who is our Home, what do you think was next on the list?

We are baptized that we might bow our knees "unto the Father of our Lord Jesus Christ, of whom the whole family in heaven and earth is named." (Ephesians 3:14-15).

After family, why do you think that active participation in the programs of the Church is important to the Savior?

Since we are all one community, do you think the Savior will be interested in how we have treated our neighbors?

How can the earth be "full of the knowledge of the Lord, as the waters cover the sea?" (Isaiah 11:9).

How does baptism prepare us for our heavenly reunion with our Father?

We are baptized that those who have died without having had the opportunity to hear about the Plan of Salvation might also partake of eternal life.

What does a "patron" do, in the House of The Lord?

What is vicarious work? (See D&C 138:33).

How does Section 2 of the Doctrine & Covenants relate to baptism for the dead?

Why do you think the wording of Malachi's prophecy is not identical in all four of the Standard Works?

135

We are baptized as a witness that "the Lord God will do nothing, but he revealeth his secret unto his servants the prophets." (Amos 3:7).

How does Section Two in The Doctrine & Covenants read?
How does the prophecy read in The Old Testament?
How does the prophecy read in The Pearl of Great Price?
How does the prophecy read in The Book of Mormon?

136

We are baptized that we might be "easy to be entreated, (and) firm to keep the commandments." (Helaman 7:7).

How can scriptural aphorisms help us to be "easily entreated?"
How can aphorisms help us to be "firm to keep the commandments?"
Would your own aphorisms help you to remember your baptismal covenant?
Can your own aphorisms help you to walk the strait and narrow way?

137 We are baptized that we might be "slow to be led to do iniquity; and quick to hearken unto the words of the Lord." (Helaman 7:7).

How does our baptism help us to be "slow to be led to do iniquity?"

What blessings do we receive when we are "quick to hearken unto the words of the Lord?"

Can those who play poker with the devil hope to win every hand?

How can hokmahs help us to remember our baptismal covenant?

138 Finally, as Ignatius Loyola declared, we are baptized that we might give and not count the cost, that we might fight and not heed the wounds, that we might toil and not seek for rest, and that we might labor and not ask for any reward save that of knowing that we do God's will.

Baptismal Prayers in The Scriptures

Doctrine & Covenants

"The person who is called of God and has authority from Jesus Christ to baptize, shall go down into the water with the person who has presented himself or herself for baptism, and shall say, calling him or her by name: Having been commissioned of Jesus Christ, I baptize you in the name of the Father, and of the Son, and of the Holy Ghost. Amen." (D&C 20:73).

Pearl of Great Price

"And he gave unto me a commandment that I should baptize in the name of the Father, and of the Son, which is full of grace and truth, and of the Holy Ghost, which beareth record of the Father and the Son." (Moses 7:11).

Book of Mormon

"Behold, ye shall go down and stand in the water, and in my name shall ye baptize them. And now behold, these are the words which ye shall say, calling them by name, saying: Having authority given me of Jesus Christ, I baptize you in the name of the Father, and of the Son, and of the Holy Ghost. Amen. And then shall ye immerse them in the water, and come forth again out of the water. And after this manner shall ye baptize in my name." (3 Nephi 11:23-27).

Holy Bible

"And Jesus came and spake unto them, saying, All power is given unto me in heaven and in earth. Go ye therefore, and teach all nations, baptizing them in the name of the Father, and of the Son, and of the Holy Ghost." (Matthew 28:18-19).

The Fourth Article of Faith

We believe that the first principles and ordinances of the Gospel are: first, Faith in the Lord Jesus Christ; second, Repentance; third, Baptism by immersion for the remission of sins; fourth, Laying on of hands for the gift of the Holy Ghost.

Bible Dictionary - Baptism

From a Greek word meaning to "dip" or "immerse." Baptism in water is the introductory ordinance of the Gospel and must be followed by baptism of the Spirit in order to be complete.

It is associated with faith in the Lord Jesus Christ, repentance, and the laying on of hands for the gift of the Holy Ghost. Baptism has always been practiced whenever the Gospel of Jesus Christ has been on the earth and has been taught by men holding the holy priesthood who could administer the ordinances.

Although there is some obscurity in the Bible as to the antiquity of baptism before the time of Jesus, from latter-day revelation it is clear that Adam was baptized (see Moses 6:64-68) and that the patriarchs and prophets since his time have taught the Gospel and administered the ordinances that pertain to the Gospel. This includes both water baptism and the laying on of hands for the Holy Ghost. (See Moses 8:23-24). The Book of Mormon also shows that baptism was taught and practiced long before the coming of Jesus Christ. (See 2 Nephi 31 and Mosiah 18:8-17).

In the New Testament, Paul speaks of the children of Israel being baptized by Moses "in the cloud and in the sea." (1 Corinthians 10:1-4). Noah and Abraham are spoken of as "preachers of righteousness," which means they taught the Gospel and administered its ordinances. (See Galatians 3:8, Hebrews 4:1-2, 2 Peter 2:5, and Moses 8:23-24).

Baptism symbolizes death, burial, and resurrection and can only be done by immersion. It is clear that John the Baptist and Philip baptized in that manner. (See Matthew 3:16, Acts 8:37-39, Romans 6:1-6, Colossians 2:12, D&C 20:72-74 & 128:12-13). Any other method is not baptism.

We learn from latter-day revelation, which confirms the teaching in the Bible, that the Aaronic Priesthood has authority to baptize with water, whereas the Melchizedek Priesthood has power to baptize not only with water but also to confer the Holy Ghost. (See D&C 13 & J.S.H. 1:68-72). We note also that John the Baptist, who had the Aaronic Priesthood, recognized this distinction and used it to illustrate one of the differences between his mission and the mission of Jesus, who had the priesthood.

Baptism is not optional if one wishes the fulness of salvation. Jesus said a person must be born of water and of the Spirit. (See John 3:3-5). When He sent forth the Twelve Apostles to teach the Gospel, He told them that whosoever believed and was baptized would be saved, and whosoever did not believe would be damned. (See Mark 16:16). Jesus Himself was baptized "to fulfil all righteousness." (See Matthew 3:15 & 2 Nephi 31:4-11). But the Pharisees, being unwilling to accept the Gospel, "rejected the counsel of God against themselves, being not baptized." (Luke 7:30).

Baptism in water has several purposes. It is for the remission of sins, for membership in the Church, and for entrance into the celestial kingdom; it is also the doorway to personal sanctification when followed by the reception of the Holy Ghost.

The age at which baptism should be administered is not specified in the Bible, although it is evident that candidates were to be old enough to be capable of belief and have some understanding. In latter-day revelation, we learn that the Lord has set the age at eight years as the time when a person begins to become accountable and can be baptized. (See D&C 20:71 & 68:25-28). This was also the age given in Old Testament times. (See J.S.T. Genesis 17:11).

Baptism is a most sacred ordinance, which a person, having received it, can remember throughout life as a reminder of the personal commitment to Jesus Christ. Its symbolism is beautiful, and its consequences ever so desirable. John the Baptist had the signal honor among all men to take the Son of God into the water and baptize Him, after which he saw the Holy Ghost descend upon Jesus. By being baptized, Jesus obeyed the law Himself and set the example for all mankind.

Topical Guide

Over 100 References to Baptism
in the Scriptures

Baptism (36)

1. Jesus, when he was baptized - Matthew 3:16
2. Baptizing them in the name of the Father - Matthew 28:19
3. John did...preach the baptism of repentance for the remission of sins - Mark 1:4
4. Baptized of John in Jordan - Mark 1:9
5. Believeth and is baptized shall be saved - Mark 16:16
6. Except a man be born of water - John 3:5
7. John also was baptizing - John 3:23
8. Repent, and be baptized - Acts 2:38
9. Into the water...and he baptized - Acts 8:38
10. Be baptized, and wash away thy sins - Acts 22:16
11. Buried with him by baptism - Romans 6:4
12. Baptized unto Moses in the cloud - 1 Corinthians 10:2
13. Baptized into Christ have put on Christ - Galatians 3:27
14. Buried with him in baptism - Colossians 2:12
15. Of the doctrine of baptisms - Hebrews 6:2
16. Even baptism doth also now save us - 1 Peter 3:21
17. Waters of Judah, or...of baptism - 1 Nephi 20:1
18. Lamb of God...baptized by water - 2 Nephi 31:5
19. Gate...is repentance and baptism by water - 2 Nephi 31:17
20. Baptized in the name of the Lord - Mosiah 18:10
21. Baptized as a witness...willing to serve God - Mosiah 21:35
22. Many were baptized in...Sidon - Alma 4:4
23. Come and be baptized unto repentance - Alma 7:14
24. After this manner shall ye baptize - 3 Nephi 11:27
25. Believeth not in me, and is not baptized, shall be damned - 3 Nephi 11:34
26. Believe...and be baptized - 3 Nephi 12:2
27. First fruits of repentance is baptism - Moroni 8:25
28. I confer...keys...of baptism - D&C 13
29. Remission of sins by baptism - D&C 19:31
30. Go ye into all the world...baptizing - D&C 68:8
31. Gospel of repentance and of baptism - D&C 874:27
32. Vicarious baptism for the remission of sins - D&C 138:33

Baptism is Essential (23)

33. Be born again...of water - Moses 6:59
34. I confer...keys...of the gospel...of baptism - J.S.H. 1:69
35. After...baptized, we experienced great and glorious blessings - J.S.H. 1:73
36. First principles...Baptism by immersion - 4th Article of Faith
37. Suffer it to be so now...to fulfil all righteousness - Matthew 3:15.
38. Teach all nations, baptizing them - Matthew 28:19
39. Jesus came...and was baptized of John - Mark 1:9
40. He that believeth and is baptized shall be saved - Mark 16:6
41. Jesus also being baptized - Luke 3:21
42. Rejected the counsel of God...being not baptized - Luke 7:30
43. Except a man be born of water...he cannot enter into the Kingdom of God - John 3:5
44. Repent, and be baptized every one of you - Acts 2:38
45. Commanded them to be baptized - Acts 10:48
46. Be baptized, and wash away thy sins - Acts 22:16
47. One Lord, one faith, one baptism - Ephesians 4:5
48. Saved us, by the washing of regeneration - Titus 3:5
49. Baptism doth also now save us - 1 Peter 3:21
50. Commandeth all men that they must...be baptized - 2 Nephi 9:23
51. Need have we, being unholy, to be baptized - 2 Nephi 31:5
52. Whoso believeth in me, and is baptized...shall be saved - 3 Nephi 11:33
53. The commandment: Repent...and be baptized - 3 Nephi 27:20
54. As many as repent and are baptized...and endure...shall be saved - D&C 18:22
55. After...baptized...a remission of your sins - D&C 55:1
56. They are they who...were baptized...according to the commandment - D&C 76:51
57. Not baptized...shall be damned - D&C 84:74
58. Turn unto me...repent...and be baptized - Moses 6:52
59. Ye must be born again...of water - Moses 6:59
60. When he was baptized, went up straightway out of the water - Matthew 3:16
61. Baptized of him in the river - Mark 1:5
62. Coming up out of the water - Mark 1:10
63. Baptizing...because there was much water there - John 3:23
64. Went down both into the water - Acts 8:38
65. Buried with him by baptism - Romans 6:4
66. One Lord, one faith, one baptism - Ephesians 4:5
67. Buried with him in baptism - Colossians 2:12
68. Were buried in the water - Mosiah 18:14
69. Immerse them in the water - 3 Nephi 11:26
70. Went down into the water and was baptized - 3 Nephi 19:11

Baptism by Immersion (17)

Qualifications for Baptism (25)

71. Had come up out of the water – 3 Nephi 19:13
72. Immerse him or her in the water – D&C 20:74
73. Baptized … being buried in the water – D&C 76:51
74. Baptism by water, to be immersed D&C 128:12
75. Laid under the water – Moses 6:64
76. Baptism by immersion – 4th Article of Faith
77. Baptized…in the river…confessing – Mark 1:5
78. He that believeth and is baptized – Mark 16:16
79. Repent, and be baptized – Acts 2:38
80. They that gladly received his word were baptized – Acts 2:41
81. If thou believest with all thine heart – Acts 8:37
82. Believe on the Lord Jesus Christ – Acts 16:31
83. The baptism of repentance – Acts 19:4
84. Be baptized…having perfect faith – 2 Nephi 9:23
85. Witnesseth…he would be obedient – 2 Nephi 31:7
86. Witness…ye have entered into a covenant – Mosiah 18:10
87. Baptized as a witness… willing to serve God – Mosiah 21:35
88. Whosoever is baptized…shall believe in my name – Mosiah 26:22
89. Who repented of their sins – Alma 6:2
90. Must repent, and be born again – Alma 7:14
91. As many as did believe were baptized – Alma 19:35
92. Whoso repenteth…and desireth to be baptized – 3 Nephi 11:23
93. Become as a little child – 3 Nephi 11:38
94. See that ye are not baptized unworthily – Mormon 9:29
95. Came forth with a broken heart and a contrite spirit – Moroni 6:2
96. Took upon them the name of Christ, having a determination to serve – Moroni 6:3
97. Who humble themselves … and desire to be baptized – D&C 20:37
98. Arrived unto the years of accountability – D&C 20:71
99. Children shall be baptized…when eight years old – D&C 68:27
100. Received the testimony of Jesus, and believed on his name – D&C 76:51
101. All men…must repent – Moses 6:57
102. What shall they do which are baptized for the dead – 1 Corinthians 15:29
103. Baptized for those who are dead – D&C 124:29
104. In relation to the baptism for your dead – D&C 127:5
105. Baptism for the dead – D&C 128:1
106. Vicarious baptism for the remission – D&C 138:33

Baptism for The Dead (5)

Brigham Young's Testimony Relating to His Baptism

"If all the talent, tact, wisdom, and refinement of the world had been sent to me with the Book of Mormon, and had declared, in the most exalted of earthly eloquence, the truth of it, undertaking to prove it by learning and worldly wisdom, they would have been to me like the smoke which arises only to vanish away. But when I saw a man without eloquence, or talents for public speaking, who could only say, 'I know, by the power of the Holy Ghost, that the Book of Mormon is true, that Joseph Smith is a Prophet of the Lord,' the Holy Ghost proceeding from that individual illuminated my understanding, and light, glory, and immortality were before me.

I was encircled by them, filled with them, and I knew for myself that the testimony of the man was true.... My own judgment, natural endowments, and education bowed to this simple, but mighty testimony. There sits the man who baptized me, brother Eleazer Miller. It filled my system with light, and my soul with joy.

The world, with all its wisdom and power, and with all the glory and gilded show of its kings or potentates, sinks into perfect insignificance, compared with the simple, unadorned testimony of the servant of God." ("Journal of Discourses," 1:91).

Lorenzo Snow's Testimony Relating to His Baptism

Lorenzo Snow was baptized and confirmed in June 1836. Recalling his developing testimony, he later said: "I believed the Latter-day Saints had the true religion, and I joined the Church. So far my conversion was merely a matter of reason." He remembered: "I was perfectly satisfied that I had done what was wisdom for me to do under the circumstances." Although he was content for a time with this understanding, he soon yearned for a special manifestation of the Holy Ghost. He said, "I had no manifestation, but I expected one."

"This manifestation did not immediately follow my baptism, as I expected," he recalled. "But, although the time was deferred, when I did receive it, its realization was more perfect, tangible and miraculous than even my strongest hopes had led me to anticipate. One day, while engaged in my studies, some two or three weeks after I was baptized, I began to reflect upon the fact that I had not obtained knowledge of the truth of the work — that I had not realized the fulfillment of the promise: 'He that doeth my will shall know of the doctrine;' and I began to feel very uneasy."

"I laid aside my books, left the house, and wandered around through the fields under the oppressive influence of a gloomy, disconsolate spirit, while an indescribable cloud of darkness seemed to envelop me. I had been accustomed, at the close of the day, to retire for secret prayer to a grove, a short distance from my lodgings, but at this time I felt no inclination to do so. The spirit of prayer had departed, and the heavens seemed like brass over my head. At length, realizing that the usual time had come for secret prayer, I concluded I would not forego my evening service, and, as a matter of formality, knelt as I was in the habit of doing, and in my accustomed retired place, but not feeling as I was wont to feel."

"I had no sooner opened my lips in an effort to pray, than I heard a sound, just above my head, like the rustling of silken robes, and immediately the Spirit of God descended upon me, completely enveloping my whole person, filling me from the crown of my head to the soles of my feet, and O, the joy and happiness I felt! No language can describe the instantaneous transition from a dense cloud of mental and spiritual darkness into a refulgence of light and knowledge, as it was at that time imparted to my understanding. I then received a perfect knowledge that God lives, that Jesus Christ is the Son of God, and of the restoration of the Holy Priesthood, and the fulness of the Gospel."

"It was a complete baptism — a tangible immersion in the heavenly principle or element, the Holy Ghost; and even more real and physical in its effects upon every part of my system than the immersion by water; dispelling forever, so long as reason and memory last, all possibility of doubt or fear in relation to the fact handed down to us historically, that the 'Babe of Bethlehem' is truly the Son of God; also the fact that He is now being revealed to the children of men, and communicating knowledge, the same as in the apostolic times. I was perfectly satisfied, as well I might be, for my expectations were more than realized, I think I may safely say, in an infinite degree."

"I cannot tell how long I remained in the full flow of this blissful enjoyment and divine enlightenment, but it was several minutes before the celestial element, which filled and surrounded me, gradually began to withdraw. On arising from my kneeling posture, with my heart swelling with gratitude to God beyond the power of expression, I felt — I knew that he had conferred on me what only an Omnipotent Being can confer — that which is of greater value than all the wealth and honors worlds can bestow." (Juvenile Instructor, January 15, 1887).

Lorenzo Snow

Phil Hudson's Testimony

I know that the Book of Mormon is the word of God through His servants the prophets to His children in the Last Days. The Spirit has repeatedly borne witness of this to me as I have feasted upon the words of this book. I testify that this companion to the Holy Bible is a second witness of Jesus Christ, and that we will draw near to God by obedience to the principles contained in this inspired work.

I know that Joseph Smith was an instrument in Heavenly Father's hands to usher in the Restoration of the Gospel of Jesus Christ and to prepare the world for the Second Coming of the Savior. It is my testimony that he was a holy apostle who held the fulness of the keys of the priesthood of God, and that by the authority given him by angelic messengers, he established The Church of Jesus Christ of Latter-day Saints.

I know that, in the words of Daniel, the Gospel will roll forth as a stone cut out of a mountain, until it fills the whole earth. I testify that missionaries have been called and set apart to preach the Gospel, that they do so with power and authority beyond their mortal capacity, and that they are saviors on Mount Zion to those who will hearken to their words.

I testify that the ordinances of the Gospel, beginning with baptism, are available to all of Heavenly Father's children.

I testify that the heavens are open, and that today God not only communicates with us through His prophets, but also that He speaks to each of us individually by the power of the Holy Ghost. I know by my own experience that the Light of Christ illuminates the way before us. I know that The Plan of Salvation is The Plan of Redemption. I know that Heavenly Father's spirit children are so important to Him that He conceived a Plan whereby they might return to His presence in the full stature of their spirits.

I know that I may one day stand before Him in spotless white garments, free of the stain of sin, because of the sacrifice of our Savior Jesus Christ. While I may not fully comprehend His Atonement, I know that it is real, because I feel my Heavenly Father's forgiveness and unconditional love when I have repented of my sins. I have felt that love ever since I was received into the Church through the portal of baptism.

It is my testimony that through my membership in The Church of Jesus Christ of Latter-day Saints, I may participate in all of the saving ordinances of the Gospel, and that, in particular, the ordinances of the temple will bind my family together forever.

I know that family exaltation in the Celestial Kingdom of God is the crown jewel of immortality and eternal life, and that God's Plan is designed to bring my family happiness in this life, and a fulness of joy in the life to come.

I know that God's Rest is within my grasp if I listen to the voice of the Spirit, am prompted to act, and endure to the end in righteousness.

Philip M. Hudson

Author's Note

Two scriptures come to mind, as I think about the ordinance of baptism.

"We talk of Christ, we rejoice in Christ, we preach of Christ, we prophesy of Christ, and we write according to our prophecies, that our children may know to what source they may look for a remission of their sins."
(2 Nephi 25:26).

"Inasmuch as parents have children in Zion, or in any of her stakes which are organized, that teach them not to understand the doctrine of repentance, faith in Christ the Son of the living God, and of baptism and the gift of the Holy Ghost by the laying on of the hands, when eight years old, the sin be upon the heads of the parents."
(D&C 68:25).

About The Author

Phil Hudson and his wife Jan have 7 children and over 20 grandchildren. They enjoy spending time with their family at their cabin nestled in the Selkirk Mountains, on the shore of Priest Lake, the crown jewel of North Idaho. Phil had a successful family dental practice in Spokane, Washington for 43 years, before retiring in 2015. He has an eclectic mix of hobbies, and enjoys riding motorcycles and ATVs. In his free time, he can be found hiking, boating, cycling, snow biking, and traveling with Jan. He always finds time, however, to record his thoughts on his laptop. He understands Isaac Asimov's response when he was asked: "If you knew that you only had 10 minutes left to live, what would you do with your time?" He answered: "I'd type faster."

When this volume was published, Phil and Jan were serving as missionaries for The Church of Jesus Christ of Latter-day Saints, in the Kingdom of Tonga. While there, they celebrated their 50th wedding anniversary.

Also By The Author

Essays

Volume One: Spray From The Ocean Of Thought

Volume Two: Ripples On A Pond

Volume Three: Serendipitous Meanderings

Volume Four: Presents Of Mind

Volume Five: Mental Floss

Volume Six: Fitness Training For The Mind And Spirit

Book of Mormon Commentary

Volume One: Born In The Wilderness

Volume Two: Voices From The Dust

Volume Three: Journey To Cumorah

Doctrine & Covenants Commentary

Volume One

Volume Two

Minute Musings: Spontaneous Combustions of Thought

Volume One

Volume Two

Volume Three

Calendars:

As I Think About The Savior
In His Own Words: Discovering William Tyndale
Scriptural Symbols

Children's Books

Muddy, Muddy
The Thirteen Articles of Faith
Happy Birthday

First Principles and Ordinances Series

Faith
Repentance
Baptism
The Holy Ghost
The Sacrament

Professional Publications

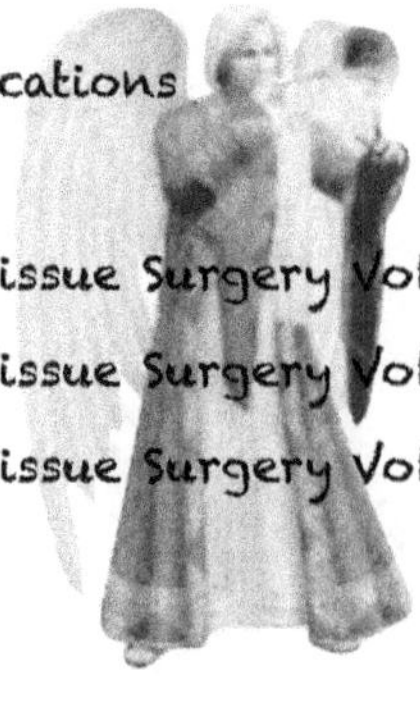

Diode Laser Soft Tissue Surgery Volume One
Diode Laser Soft Tissue Surgery Volume Two
Diode Laser Soft Tissue Surgery Volume Three

These, and other titles, are available from online retailers.

Quid tibi ego alia narrem?

www.ingramcontent.com/pod-product-compliance
Lightning Source LLC
Chambersburg PA
CBHW060507240426
43661CB00007B/940